Y0-CKM-107

1,000 Prayers for Difficult Times

Inspiration for When You Don't Know What to Pray

© 2018 by Barbour Publishing, Inc.

ISBN 978-1-68322-723-6

All rights reserved. No part of this publication may be reproduced or transmitted for commercial purposes, except for brief quotations in printed reviews, without written permission of the publisher.

Some text previously appeared in the following: *Prayers for Difficult Times*, *Prayers for Difficult Times Women's Edition*, *Prayers for Difficult Times Men's Edition*, and *Prayers for Difficult Times: Cancer*, all published by Barbour Publishing.

Churches and other noncommercial interests may reproduce portions of this book without the express written permission of Barbour Publishing, provided that the text does not exceed 500 words or 5 percent of the entire book, whichever is less, and that the text is not material quoted from another publisher. When reproducing text from this book, include the following credit line: "From *1,000 Prayers for Difficult Times*, published by Barbour Publishing, Inc. Used by permission."

Scripture quotations marked NKJV are taken from the New King James Version®. Copyright © 1982 by Thomas Nelson, Inc. Used by permission. All rights reserved.

Scripture quotations marked NIV are taken from the HOLY BIBLE, NEW INTERNATIONAL VERSION®. NIV®. Copyright © 1973, 1978, 1984, 2011 by Biblica, Inc.™ Used by permission. All rights reserved worldwide.

Scripture quotations marked MSG are from *THE MESSAGE*. Copyright © by Eugene H. Peterson 1993, 1994, 1995, 1996, 2000, 2001, 2002. Used by permission of NavPress Publishing Group.

Scripture quotations marked NLT are taken from the *Holy Bible*. New Living Translation copyright© 1996, 2004, 2015 by Tyndale House Foundation. Used by permission of Tyndale House Publishers, Inc. Carol Stream, Illinois 60188. All rights reserved.

Scripture quotations marked ESV are from The Holy Bible, English Standard Version®, copyright © 2001 by Crossway Bibles, a publishing ministry of Good News Publishers. Used by permission. All rights reserved.

Scripture quotations marked KJV are taken from the King James Version of the Bible.

Scripture quotations marked ASV are taken from the American Standard Version of the Bible.

Scripture quotations marked NASB are taken from the New American Standard Bible, © 1960, 1962, 1963, 1968, 1971, 1972, 1973, 1975, 1977, 1995 by The Lockman Foundation. Used by permission.

Scripture quotations marked NCV are taken from the New Century Version of the Bible, copyright © 2005 by Thomas Nelson, Inc. Used by permission. All rights reserved.

Published by Barbour Books, an imprint of Barbour Publishing, Inc., 1810 Barbour Drive, Uhrichsville, Ohio 44683, www.barbourbooks.com

Our mission is to inspire the world with the life-changing message of the Bible.

Member of the
Evangelical Christian
Publishers Association

Printed in China.

1,000 Prayers for Difficult Times

Inspiration for When You Don't Know What to Pray

BARBOUR BOOKS
An Imprint of Barbour Publishing, Inc.

CONTENTS

Introduction 7
1. Abuse 8
2. Accidents 14
3. Addiction 19
4. Adultery 24
5. Alcohol Abuse 30
6. Anger 34
7. Anxiety 41
8. Arguments 47
9. Bankruptcy 52
10. Bargaining with God 55
11. Betrayal 57
12. Bitterness 62
13. Challenges 65
14. Chronic Illness 70
15. Chronic Pain 75
16. Church Discord 79
17. Crying Out to God 84
18. Death of a Child 86
19. Death of a Parent 91
20. Death of a Pet 96
21. Death of a Spouse 102
22. Denial 107
23. Depression 109
24. Disabilities 114
25. Disappointment 119
26. Discontentment 124
27. Dishonesty 127
28. Distrust 131
29. Divorce/Separation 136
30. Doubt 141
31. Drug Abuse 146
32. Dysfunctional Relationships 151
33. Elderly Parents 156
34. Emotional and Spiritual Pain 160
35. Emotional and Spiritual Weakness 162
36. Enemies 164
37. Facing Death 169
38. Failure 175
39. Family Feuds 180

40. Family Stress 184
41. Fear 188
42. Financial Strain 192
43. Foreclosure 197
44. Gambling 200
45. Going through Change 202
46. Greed 205
47. Grief 208
48. Guilt 212
49. Helplessness 215
50. Hidden Sin 220
51. Hopelessness 224
52. Infertility 228
53. Injustice 235
54. Insomnia 239
55. Isolation and Loneliness 243
56. Jealousy 245
57. Job Loss 248
58. Job Stress 251
59. Leadership 256
60. Litigation 258
61. Loneliness 261
62. Marital Strife/ Dysfunction 264

63. Moving 267
64. Overwhelmed 270
65. Physical Pain 273
66. Physical Weakness 276
67. Pornography 278
68. Praise in the Midst of the Worst 280
69. Prodigal Children 282
70. Regret 287
71. Self-Esteem 290
72. Sexual Identity 293
73. Shame 296
74. Sickness 300
75. Singleness 302
76. Surgery 305
77. Terror 309
78. Toxic Friendships 312
79. Unforgiveness 316
80. Violence 319
81. Weakness 324
82. Worry 328

INTRODUCTION

*Give all your worries and cares to God,
for he cares about you.*
1 PETER 5:7 NLT

Prayer doesn't miraculously take away life's challenges. It's not a magic formula that whisks our troubles away. Jesus Himself prayed to be delivered from the cross—and yet through prayer, He also accepted that this was God's will for Him. The apostle Paul prayed to be delivered from "his thorn in the flesh"—but when God did not remove this trouble from his life, Paul allowed God to use it to make him stronger. Prayer was the way both Jesus and Paul struggled with their emotional reactions to life's difficulties. It allowed them to transform the meaning of their circumstances, so that what had been a crisis became an opportunity for God's creative work.

Prayer can do the same for us. As it opens us up to God's Spirit, we will see Him working through us and in us. Prayer will bring us peace even in the midst of the most difficult times.

Use these prayer starters as jumping-off points for your own prayers. Many of them are based on scripture. A few are prayers from the old saints of our faith. All of them can be used as "conversation starters" between your heart and God's!

ABUSE

This means that anyone who belongs to Christ has become a new person. The old life is gone; a new life has begun!
2 Corinthians 5:17 nlt

◆

Abuse is a topic that's hard to talk about openly. Whether it's something that lies long ago in our past—or it's something we or our friends are dealing with today in the present—the shame that goes along with this topic is hard to face.

But God wants to take away that sense of shame. He wants us to understand that in His eyes, we are clean and pure. Abuse tells lies. It says that the abused person is unworthy of love and dignity and respect. God longs to smash those lies with the love and truth of Christ's Gospel.

In Christ, we are new people. He is waiting to help us walk away from abuse—into a new life.

Lord God, I am trying to face a fearful reality: I may be an abusive spouse. I've threatened, isolated, and withheld my affection, support, and resources. I've failed the person You gave me to love and cherish. Help me rebuild what I've damaged, one day, one moment at a time.

◇◇◇

Help me this day to see the lies others have told me about myself as what they are—lies. Remind me of the truth that I am fearfully and wonderfully made in Your image and that You have great plans for my future.

◇◇◇

Lord, I know I am precious in Your eyes. I am beautiful and spotless in Your sight. Help me to hold my head high, wrapped in the knowledge that I am Your child. Take away my shame. Heal my wounded memories. Create something new inside me. Make me whole again, I pray.

◇◇◇

Jesus, I feel alone at times when I think about what has been done to me. I wonder if it's somehow my fault. Thank You for reassuring me time after time that it's not my fault and that You are here with me even in my darkest hour. Help me to sense Your presence now, I pray. You are my Savior, and You have promised to never leave me. What a wonderful promise!

◇◇◇

In my own power, I know I could never rise above this. But in You, all things are possible. Help me to feel safe and whole again. Give me peace and joy once more. I claim these things my birthright as Your child. Thank You.

Jesus, You have called me to be gentle and loving toward my wife: "Husbands, love your wives and never treat them harshly" (Colossians 3:19 NLT). I have not obeyed You. Help me to break from my negative thoughts and actions and to become more like You. Taken to extremes, my perfectionism becomes criticism, my jealousy becomes obsession, and my competitiveness becomes domination. I know You have a better, higher way for me—to be merciful and humble, to treat my wife with respect and kindness.

◇◇◇

God, I'm afraid when I see a certain person or type of person. I feel the fear wash over me again. I keep thinking I've put the memories behind me, but then there they are again. I feel the sting of abuse as fresh as the times when it occurred. Please take control of my thoughts and cast out Satan and his desire to pull me down.

◇◇◇

I don't feel very loveable, God. It's hard for me to believe that You really love me. I'm afraid of being intimate, even with You. I'm afraid to let down the barriers I've built around my heart. Help me to trust You.

◇◇◇

Heavenly Father, I look back and I see the pain but also Your provision. I see the way You took me out of yesterday and brought me into today, Father. In the Bible, Your people built altars as reminders. I call to mind in this moment the ways in which You have rescued me. I thank You for the people who have helped me. I read in Your Word of Your great love for me. Continue to heal my heart, I pray, in ways that only You can.

I know You are on my side, Lord. You want me to be whole.
You want me to trust You so that I can receive Your blessings.
You want to give me the capacity to walk in Your grace
and wrap myself in Your love. You are the Creator
of the world. There is nothing too hard for You!

◇◇◇

Father, I feel so vulnerable. I fear being hurt again. I know that I can't hide behind walls. Help me to trust You, Lord, and give me wisdom about the people I can trust. Show me safe people, God.

◇◇◇

I love the verse in scripture that says the battle is the Lord's. My battle is not with weapons or against a large army, but it feels every bit as challenging! I fight a battle to love myself and to forgive the ones who have hurt me. I fight it every day. I'm thankful that the battle is Yours, Jesus. I can't do it on my own.

◇◇◇

Father, Your Word says that I am to love my wife "as Christ loved the church and gave himself up for her" (Ephesians 5:25 NIV). But even though I am a Christian, I am not Christ. I'm forgiven but still capable of falling—and that's what I've done with my wife. I've been harsh, unforgiving, and merciless with her. I am ashamed. I want to run, to ignore the problem, to shift the blame—but I can't. Please forgive me and give me the courage to seek both her forgiveness and accountability from a church leader.

◇◇◇

I am Yours, and that's enough today, Jesus. I belong to
the Messiah, the Savior of the world. This world has
its troubles, but I know that with You in my heart,
I can survive. We've got this!

Jesus, I know You came to heal the brokenhearted. Heal my broken heart, I pray. You came to deliver captives into freedom. Set me free from abuse. You came to heal those who are bruised. I ask that You heal the scars of abuse in my heart, in my mind and memories, and in my life. Please rescue me!

◇◇◇

Jesus, my old abusive habits are tempting me today. Fill me with Your Spirit so that I won't belittle or criticize my wife or my children but build them up instead. Bring to mind what it looks like to be near me when I act badly—not so that I get stuck in the past, but so I can remember the cost of my sin. I am sick over what I've done, and it still nags at me. Help me, Lord, to make that extra effort to be loving and kind, even if I need to isolate myself until I am under control again. Let me live with my wife "in an understanding way" (1 Peter 3:7 ESV), and let me nourish and cherish her the way You nourish and cherish the church (Ephesians 5:28–29). Help me to guide my children "in the training and instruction of the Lord" (Ephesians 6:4 NIV) and to avoid exasperating them and provoking them to wrath (v. 4 NKJV).

◇◇◇

God, I can't face this situation all alone. I know You are always with me—but please send someone else to help me, someone who will give me support and guidance, who will help me take the steps I need to deal with this situation. I'm not strong enough to do this on my own.

I feel so many things, Lord. I feel guilt. . .grief. . .fear. . .anger. All these emotions are mixed up inside me. Sometimes I wonder how I can ever get past them. And yet I believe that even in this, You are making me into the person You want me to be. Somehow—even in the midst of all this pain— You are working all things together for my good.

◇◇◇

Father, my wife is dealing with the effects of someone else's abuse. Help me to make our relationship a secure place, and empower me to avoid reacting to her stress and anger with my own. Even though I am surprised and heartbroken to find this out, help me to look past my own shock and seize the opportunity to begin to heal. I want to be like Joseph, who didn't understand the situation with Mary but still let his compassion and love for her guide his behavior toward her. Please heal my wife, and let me be part of that healing— especially when it's difficult, when it affects our sex life and our friendship. I want to take the long view and trust You with the daily details.

ACCIDENTS

And we know that in all things God works for the good of those who love him, who have been called according to his purpose.
ROMANS 8:28 NIV

When an accident happens, we're suddenly struck with how fragile our lives are. There we are, going along like normal, when without warning, something bad happens. Our sense of safety and security shatters. Life feels shaky, as though unexpected danger is lurking around every corner. It's hard to regain a sense of peace.

But God's love is powerful and creative. The same amazing divine energy that made the world is still at work in each and every event of our lives. What seems like catastrophe will be swept up by His power and made into something that ultimately, in some way we may not be able to even imagine now, will bless us and those we love.

True faith in God doesn't mean that we believe nothing bad will ever happen to us. Instead, it means we trust God to use even the bad things for our good and His glory.

Lord God, what happened makes me feel foolish and frustrated. Please give me Your perspective. Even if I can't see past my own part in the accident or understand why You let it happen, You can help me focus on You. I trust that You can make something good come out of this setback.

◇◇◇

Father, Your Word tells us that You have an appointed time for everything. From Your perspective, there are no accidents. You never get the timing wrong. Help me to trust Your plan for my life.

◇◇◇

Father, I know that there is a time for everything. Your Word tells me this. I don't understand how this could be part of Your plan, but I pray You will use even this for Your glory. May I look back one day in the future and see how Your hand was at work in my life even though it was a very difficult time.

◇◇◇

God, I know Your works are perfect. You don't make mistakes. I believe You know what You're doing, even now, when I'm in the midst of disaster.

◇◇◇

Since You watch over the sparrows, loving Lord, help me to know that You are all the more aware of the events in my life. You never sleep, the psalmist wrote, so nothing takes You by surprise. I rely on You.

◇◇◇

God, I know that You are in control. Just as You care for the sparrows and the lilies of the field, You take care of my needs. I am Your child. You will never take Your hand off my life.

Father, this accident has turned my life upside down. It helps me understand what David meant when he wrote about not being able to sleep at night because of his anxiety. Like him, "I am weary with my groaning" (Psalm 6:6 NKJV). And like David, I ask, "O LORD, heal me, for my bones are troubled. My soul also is greatly troubled" (vv. 2–3 NKJV).

◇◇◇

I sometimes feel the shock I experienced after the accident. It seems like I'm living it again. Instead of shock, envelop me in peace, stability, and calm. You brought me through, and You will continue to do so. . .day by day.

◇◇◇

God, my world seems upside down. And yet I trust You. The timing couldn't be worse. And yet I trust You. I am overwhelmed with emotion and weariness as I try to deal with these events. And yet I trust You.

◇◇◇

God, in Your Word it seems like You are always turning bad things into good things. You struck down Saul on the road to Damascus only to raise him up as a great leader. You brought a flood, but when it was over, You made the world into a better place. Use this accident. Use this pain. Create a new thing here, and cause me to see and appreciate it.

◇◇◇

This just wasn't how I wanted things to go, Father. I can't believe this actually happened and that I'm sitting here in the midst of what seems impossible to overcome. Give me strength to face the mountains ahead, because in You, all things are possible. Even healing. Even moving forward from this hardship.

Father, my guilt over my part in this accident is eating me up. Others have suffered because of something I did. It doesn't help that I didn't mean for it to happen either. Forgive me, and comfort those this incident affects. Please help me figure out what to do—if I should make restitution or work toward restoring relationships, I'm willing. I trust Your timing, Your sovereignty, and that You can make good come out of bad.

◇◇◇

I wake up in the night, Father, troubled and scared. I'm so shaken by this tragedy, and I feel like I will never be the same. Remind me that I can lie down and rest peacefully because You are watching over me. I ask this in the powerful name of Jesus who heals.

◇◇◇

The psalmist wrote that You go before me on my path—and You follow after me. That means You were waiting for me there in the middle of what looked to me like such a terrible accident— and now that it's over, You're here with me still, helping me to pick up the pieces. Help me be willing to build something new in the wake of this disaster, with Your help.

◇◇◇

Dear Lord, You are all-seeing, all-knowing, all-powerful, all-loving. You always have my best in mind. And in You there are no "accidents."

◇◇◇

You did not look away or forget us, God. You were there. Help me to trust that Your ways are higher than mine and Your thoughts are higher than my thoughts. Dear Lord, You are omnipotent and omnipresent. You always have my best in mind.

It's hard for me to go on now, Creator God. I lie awake at night, burdened with anxiety. When I slip into unconsciousness at last, nightmares trouble my sleep. Restore my peace, I pray. Teach me to rest once more in the shadow of Your wings. I know that You let nothing touch me that has not first passed through Your loving hands.

◇◇◇

God, these are hard days. I wake up to the sun shining through my window, and I wonder how it could be so bright and pretty outside when I feel so sad and sick inside. I know that it may take time, but I pray that You will restore in my heart a sense of joy. And for today, Lord, will You carry me? Will You please remind me that You are so very close and that You have not—and will not *ever*—let me go?

◇◇◇

God, You are perfect in all Your ways (Psalm 18:30). You are blameless and Your Word is tried and true. You are my shield and my refuge. Your timing is always just right. Help me keep my eyes on You. Make something good come out of this hot mess. This is who You are, and this is what You do.

ADDICTION

It is for freedom that Christ has set us free. Stand firm, then, and do not let yourselves be burdened again by a yoke of slavery.
GALATIANS 5:1 NIV

Addiction is a form of slavery. It makes us need some substance or activity to get through life—to the point that our need is a compulsion that overpowers our other responsibilities and relationships, and even our health. We may not realize how big the problem is, but sooner or later, we wake up to the fact that addiction has become the master. No matter what we believe intellectually about God, addiction becomes our real god. We no longer rely on the Creator of the universe for help with life's challenges. Instead, we cannot face stress or sorrow, weariness or anger, without turning to our addiction.

But God wants to set us free. Jesus came to break the bonds of slavery—including the slavery of addiction!

I see my addiction for what it is—a false face I've tried to put on to deal with my problems. I want to see Your face, and I want to live my whole life like You are right here next to me. I commit myself to living in integrity before You—to consistently walking in a pattern of thoughts, words, and deeds that bring true life. . .and that open my heart to You.

◇◇◇

Each day is a new start. Help me this day to resist the temptation to take an easier way out. Help me to stay the course. God, my addiction causes me nothing but sickness and grief. Remind me that Your ways are pure and good and that they always bring me out on top.

◇◇◇

Father, I can't do this on my own. Please place in my path the right counselor, group, or program. I pray that You will guide my steps and give me the strength to walk in the right direction.

◇◇◇

I am a new creation in You, Jesus. I thought that would mean that I'm no longer tempted. I thought I would wake up a changed person and ready to face life addiction-free, but I'm still struggling. Walk with me. Show me the way. Help me to trust Your timing as You heal me and set me free.

◇◇◇

Lord God, I've sacrificed so much to my addiction—time, resources, relationships. Help me to be a "living sacrifice" (Romans 12:1 NIV) so I can redeem all those things. Fill me with Your Spirit, make Your Word come alive for me, and help me to find godly counsel and accountability. You are for me, God, so who can be against me?

I wish that I could wave a magic wand and cause the one I love to walk away from this addiction. I feel like I have to compete with it day and night. I can't change the situation, but I can bring it to You in prayer. I put this whole thing into Your strong and capable hands, heavenly Father. I ask that You change what I cannot.

◇◇◇

Jesus, I carry a cross every day. It is a sick addiction that brings me nothing good. It offers nothing beneficial to anyone in my life. It only brings pain, pain, and more pain. I will carry this cross. I will seek to be entirely free of it one day, but if it's always there in the back of my mind, let it be a thing of the past and not something that continues to destroy my present and my future.

◇◇◇

Lord, You know I want to change. And yet again and again, I fall back into the same addictive behaviors. I get so discouraged with myself. Thank You, Lord, that You are never discouraged with me. You are always waiting to give me one more chance.

◇◇◇

I remember a line from the children's song "Jesus Loves Me" that says "I am weak but He is strong." That rings so true today. I thought I could beat this thing anytime I wanted—all by myself. I was so wrong. I need You, Lord, to help me stay sober. I need You every minute of every day. I am weak, but hallelujah—You are strong!

◇◇◇

Help me, Lord, to look deep into my heart and examine my ways. Show me where I hurt those I love—my parents, my spouse, my children, my friends. Help me to take an honest inventory of my life. I want to change. I need Your help.

Help me to surrender and lay my addiction down at Your feet, Father. I have to keep starting over. I feel like a failure. Be the lifter of my head. Be my defender against the enemy who wants to keep me captive in this addiction.

◇◇◇

Father, I can't do this without support. Show me where I should turn. Lead me to the right counselor, the right group, the right program. I want to change. Show me how.

◇◇◇

God, I feel my addiction pulling on me today. Right now, I want so badly to do the thing I used to do that I can't even think straight. Help me to remember You. You are my goal and my reward. I know I need endurance, so that when I have done Your will, I may receive Your reward (Hebrews 10:36). "We are not of those who shrink back and are destroyed, but of those who have faith and preserve their souls" (v. 39 ESV). Pull me toward You.

◇◇◇

I don't want to be double-minded—trying to get both what You want *and* what I want. What I do know is that I can't overcome my addiction—but *You can*. I want to be patient, just like You are with me, and committed to obeying You. I will seek You each day—each *moment*, if necessary—from now on.

◇◇◇

I am so weak, God. But You promised me that Your power is made perfect in weakness, that Your grace is all I need. Here, God. I put my weakness in Your hands. Use it however You want. May Your grace fill my life.

I can't change the people I love, God, no matter how much I love them. Only You can do that. You know how this addiction in my loved one's life hurts me, how much I wish I could do something, how helpless I feel. I give my feelings to You. I give my loved one to You. I give this entire situation to You. I trust You to bring Your healing power to my loved one's life.

◇◇◇

Jesus, in the Gospels, You said that if I want to be Your follower, I have to be willing to take up my cross each day and then walk in Your footsteps. I claim this addiction as the cross I carry. I pick it up in Your name. I may never be free of it. But I believe You have a plan for my life, and I know You will give me the strength to carry it.

◇◇◇

Father, cut me off from the things that tempt me, and from the means I use to fulfill them—suppliers, resources, the internet, social media, bad company. When I slip and fall, help me get back up and try again. Because my sin hurts me, I know that Your Spirit is working in me. You won't give up on me, but please help me not to give up on myself. I know You will deliver me through Jesus Christ.

◇◇◇

I know that the Twelve Steps of Alcoholics Anonymous requires a "searching and fearless moral inventory." It's hard for me to undertake such a terrifying task. I'd rather not look at who and what I am. But, Lord, You also ask me to examine my ways and test them, so that I can truly return to Your presence. So give me the strength and courage I need. I am ready to be obedient to Your will.

ADULTERY

"You know the next commandment pretty well, too: 'Don't go to bed with another's spouse.' But don't think you've preserved your virtue simply by staying out of bed. Your heart can be corrupted by lust even quicker than your body. Those leering looks you think nobody notices—they also corrupt."
MATTHEW 5:27–28 MSG

We all know the technical definition of adultery, but Jesus pointed out that it's not quite that simple. If we take a look at the root meanings for the word *adultery*, here's what we come up with: the oldest meanings of the word meant "to spoil, to break, to destroy." So any time we let something break our marriage vows, destroy our relationship with our spouse, or spoil the intimacy we share, we have opened the door to adultery. Jesus said that even something as seemingly harmless as ogling someone other than our partner could damage our marriage! God asks us to protect married love, to set a shelter around it that keeps out anything that could threaten it.

Father, I see my unfaithfulness for what it truly is—sin. And first and foremost, I've sinned against You. Forgive me for all the excuses I've made to justify my behavior. Nothing my spouse has done justifies my actions. The thought of directly confessing my unfaithfulness terrifies me, but I understand that I need to do it. I also understand that there is biblical justification if my spouse chooses to end our marriage. Give me the courage to do what is right—and to continue to do what is right from now on. Please save our marriage.

◇◇◇

God, my spouse wasn't faithful to me, but expresses a desire to be now. I don't know how to respond. Give me wisdom. Grant me the ability to face these decisions and difficulties which seem so insurmountable to me. I never dreamed I would end up here. I'm glad You have not left me, even now.

◇◇◇

I was unfaithful. How could I have done these things and been untrue to my spouse? I feel like I've committed the unforgivable sin. Yet You tell me in Your Word You can forgive any sin through the blood of Jesus shed on the cross. I know the words, but I pray You will help them reach deep into my heart where I can somehow forgive myself. I don't like who I've become, and I pray for supernatural change in my life that can only come about through Your grace and forgiveness.

◇◇◇

God, I stayed true to my spouse—but my spouse was unfaithful to me. How can I forgive? How can I ever trust again? How can I even try to rebuild this broken marriage? Lord, give me wisdom to face the future. Show me Your way. Heal my heart.

Lord, I am casting blame. Every day I wake up blaming the one who betrayed me. The blame is starting to eat at me and build a fortress of bitterness in my very spirit. It's affecting everything I do. . .every word I speak. It's dragging me down to a low, low place. Remove the blame from my heart. Remind me that I am far from perfect and that I'm not free from fault in this. Show me areas where I need to change, and soften my heart where it needs to be softened, I ask in Your name.

◇◇◇

Help me, Jesus, to lay this burden down at Your feet. I read about how You called on those men gathered around the adulterous woman to throw the first stone if they were without sin. I am not without sin. Forgive me, Father, and help me to forgive.

◇◇◇

I failed my spouse, God. How can I forgive myself? How can I ever hope to be trustworthy again? How can I begin to rebuild what my own hands have broken? I pray that You would give me wisdom, Lord. Show me Your way. Heal me, heal my spouse, heal our marriage. Give us hope for the future.

◇◇◇

Sweet Jesus, I am broken. Where once there was trust, there is distrust. Where once there was intimacy, I feel stone cold. Show me the way forward. Make it clear, I pray. I need You now like never before. I can't get through this on my own.

Lord God, right now I hurt so bad I can barely breathe. I know I need to love my spouse the way You love me—sacrificially, in spite of my sin—but all I can think about is the sin that was committed against me. Forgive me for my thoughts of what I'd like to do to the person who took part in the cheating. I know vengeance is Yours, not mine (Hebrews 10:30). I don't know if I can forgive them without Your help, but I know it's what You want me to do. Calm the whirling of my thoughts and the churning of my gut. Give me Your heart, Lord, because mine is broken.

◇◇◇

Dear heavenly Father, You were there. You saw my unfaithfulness. Let's call it what it was. Adultery. You know my sin, and yet You love me still. Tears stream down my face. My heart hurts so deeply with something I can never take back. Help me to never make this mistake again.

◇◇◇

I know the voice of my Shepherd. I have been listening to it for many years. I am being called upon in a way I never knew possible to tune into that voice and seek direction only from the One who knows me best. Give me grace for the moment and the healing and power to get through this, Lord.

◇◇◇

Father, even though I'm heartbroken at what my spouse has done, I know I haven't been perfect. You told us to forgive others because You've forgiven us (Ephesians 4:32), and You tell us to "make allowance for each other's faults" (Colossians 3:13 NLT). As we go through counseling and learning to live with each other in light of what's happened, let Your love and grace flow through me. I need Your peace desperately, through all the ups and downs.

Lord, I wasn't physically unfaithful, not in the way that my spouse was unfaithful to me. But remind me that I am not perfect either. Allow me to see how I have failed my spouse. Remove my self-righteous indignation and reveal to me all the ways I too have hurt the one I love. Teach us both humility, so that we can begin to forgive each other.

◇◇◇

Help me, Jesus, to accept all the ways I am at fault. Remind me not to evade my own guilt by blaming my spouse for my actions. Help me to be strong enough to accept the consequences of what I've done. I know that all I can do now is give the past to You. Teach me humility, I pray.

◇◇◇

God, I opened the door to something that turned me against my spouse—bitterness or lust or emotional absence—and I poisoned my heart. I haven't yet acted on it physically, but I have indulged the thought of cheating. You've made it clear that I've already been unfaithful (Matthew 5:27–28), and I need to confess my sin to my loved one. I need Your strength to do that, and I need Your Spirit to help me find the words and to receive the reaction. Help me to make "a covenant with my eyes" (Job 31:1 NIV). I commit to staying true to my spouse, to breaking contact with the sources of my temptation—the other person, social media, second looks, flirting at work, looking at porn—whatever I need to do to heal our hearts and our marriage.

Loving Lord, how can I get past this? My sense of security and
my trust have been broken. The intimacy and privacy I thought
I shared with my spouse have been invaded. I want to forgive—
and yet I'm scared. I can't get past the lies I was told. I don't
know how to begin rebuilding our marriage when I
feel as though I would be stupid to ever trust
again. Show me the way forward, I pray.

◇◇◇

Dear God, You know how badly I hurt my spouse.
Remind me I must give my partner time to grieve, time to
heal. Keep me patient. Teach me to wait—and to stay
committed to the future while I wait. Create a new heart
in me, so that one day my spouse will trust me once more.

◇◇◇

You understand us, Lord. You know what we are facing.
You have a plan for us. Your Spirit longs to lead us forward
into a future of hope and love and strength. We trust in You.

◇◇◇

God, I've been unfaithful to my spouse. I've confessed it,
and we are getting help to deal with the pain I've caused.
We both have things to work on. Strengthen us to love
each other, to show grace, to forgive, and to keep
our hearts set on You. Heal our relationship.

ALCOHOL ABUSE

But the fruit of the Spirit is. . .self-control. . . . Those who belong to Christ Jesus have crucified the flesh with its passions and desires. Since we live by the Spirit, let us keep in step with the Spirit.

GALATIANS 5:22–25 NIV

When we abuse alcohol, our relationships suffer. Our physical health suffers. We have less energy for the people and activities we care about most. And most of all, our relationship with God suffers.

God wants us at our best, emotionally, physically, intellectually, socially. Alcohol abuse gets in the way of this. It's not that God is a goody-goody teetotaler! But our deepest connections with Him can only thrive when we are becoming the people He created us to be. He doesn't want anything to hinder that—including alcohol.

Lord, I need Your wisdom and strength to avoid situations
and people that compromise my commitment to follow You
and stop drinking. Help me to recognize the triggers that push
me to drink—the stress or exhaustion or whatever it may be.
I want to learn to take care of myself, physically and
spiritually, but I can't do it without You.

◇◇◇

Dear Lord, I'm learning that some situations are harder
for me to handle than others. When I'm with certain people,
for example, I'm more likely to drink too much. When
I allow myself to become emotionally and physically
drained, I'm also more likely to turn to alcohol. I could use
Your help with this, God! Could You remind me *before* I'm
in the situation to protect myself? Help me avoid the social
gatherings where I'm likely to drink more than is good for me.

◇◇◇

Jesus, give me the courage to seek help. I've hit rock bottom
many times, and it's clear to me that I can't quit drinking on my
own. I need Your help, but I also need accountability—strong
Christians who can support and encourage me to switch my
dependency over to You. I feel like I need to relearn how to live
without alcohol. Fill me with Your Spirit and make me hungry
for Your Word. Teach me how to die to myself and follow You.

◇◇◇

Setting boundaries is so hard for me, Lord. I feel guilty
whenever I try to draw a line around myself, whenever I say
this far and no farther. Give me wisdom to know which
lines need to be drawn, I pray. Give me courage
to set boundaries—and then stick to them.

Help me this day, Father, to be wise rather than
foolish. Help me to refrain from drinking, which leads
me to do things that are not pleasing to You.
Help me instead to be filled with Your Holy Spirit.

◇◇◇

Where did this addiction come from, and why does it have such
a hold on me? I pray for the ability to see it for what it is
today, Lord. A problem. Admitting it is the first step.

◇◇◇

I know You are helping me, Jesus. I believe You are with me.
Please send human helpers too. Give me the courage to let
others know I have this problem—and then to ask for their help.

◇◇◇

God, I want to be a person of character and integrity,
not someone who sneaks around finding my next drink.
I want my life to be pleasing to You, and I want to be ready
when You come back to take me home (Romans 13:11–13).
Remind me of Your love—and that You died for me while I was
still a sinner (Romans 5:8). You know what I am, but You still
see me as worth the cost of Your only begotten Son to redeem. I
don't understand that kind of love, but I want it desperately.

◇◇◇

Forgive me, and help me recommit to sobriety, right now.
Please provide for me just the right helpers,
people who are like me, people who have escaped this
prison and have begun a new life free from alcohol.

I have made alcohol my god—although I never meant to.
It's such a pitiful god. It offers me nothing. Please intervene
in this drama I have created for myself. Draw me back to a
place of safety where pleasant borders are established
in my life (Psalm 16:6). I love You, Lord.

◇◇◇

When I'm stressed, God, it's so easy to reach for a drink.
Just one—I tell myself—won't hurt. But then I find myself
thinking, One *more* is all right. And then before I know it,
I realize I've done it again. I've turned to alcohol as the
crutch to carry my tension. When I'm sober again,
the stress is still there, of course. I never seem to learn.

◇◇◇

I didn't see myself as sick for a long time, but now
I am beginning to. This is an illness. I need Your
divine intervention. I need You to show up
as the Great Physician in my life.

◇◇◇

I need Your help with this, Father God. I need You to help
me find new ways of coping, ways that bring me closer to You.
When I'm overwhelmed by life, teach me instead to exercise,
to sing, to call someone on the phone, to do something creative,
to take a nap. Whatever else You lead me to, be at its center.
Use my feelings of stress as the trigger that tells me: Time to pray.

◇◇◇

Father, I've fallen again. I lied to myself, telling myself that one
little drink wouldn't hurt. But I don't drink to do anything
but get drunk, and I can feel the distance it creates between
You and me. I hate it, and I'm fighting not to hate myself.

ANGER

*Stop being angry! Turn from your rage!
Do not lose your temper—it only leads to harm.*
PSALM 37:8 NLT

We all get angry from time to time. But the Bible tells us to not nurse our anger. Instead of dwelling on it, the psalmist says that we should turn away from it. Instead of feeding it until we explode, we are to let it go. There's nothing wrong with feeling angry sometimes—but when we let our anger drive us, when we lose control of ourselves because we're so full of rage, then we're likely to hurt those around us.

Acknowledge your angry feelings. Don't try to stuff them away or deny that they exist. But then give them to God. Allow Him to be the container that holds your temper—and keeps it from hurting others.

Remind me, Father, that You have made me new in Christ. I am a new creation (2 Corinthians 5:17), and You have redeemed me from the curse of sin (Galatians 3:13). You will complete the good work You started in me (Philippians 1:6), and I am Your "workmanship, created in Christ Jesus for good works, which [You] prepared beforehand that [I] should walk in them" (Ephesians 2:10 NKJV). Knowing these things, I can choose what to do when I get angry. I can put that energy into making things right or addressing injustice—and I don't have to lose my cool, because You are with me.

◇◇◇

Dear God, I know that anger lives in pain. Where there is hurt in my life, I often react in anger. Things explode from my mouth that I regret later. Please heal the pain in me and set a guard over my tongue so that I will not hurt others in my anger.

◇◇◇

Jesus, when You got angry, it was a righteous anger. I get angry when things don't go my way or when others say or do things to hurt me. Help me not to be so egocentric. Help me to be kingdom centered.

◇◇◇

Lord, James 1:19–20 sums it up. I want to be quick to listen to what others have to say, slow to speak, and even slower to lose my temper. Please help me to take Your Word into my heart and allow it to transform me.

Lord God, so many things make me angry—disrespect, incompetence, selfishness, messiness, lack of consideration—but abdicating my control only makes me more likely provoked to anger since others fail to meet my expectations without my oversight. I need Your wisdom to understand which offenses are real and which ones are only perceived. And then, I need to let go of the perceived ones with grace and forgiveness, and deal with the real ones with respectful honesty, sympathy, and understanding.

◇◇◇

When I hear the whisper that You are doing this to punish me, because You are not really a God of love after all, reassure me that this whisper comes not from Your Spirit but from Satan, the father of lies.

◇◇◇

God, I'm mad at You! Why did You let this happen? I know I should calm down and trust You—but my anger is just too big. I can't give You praise right now. I can't sing worship songs. The only thing I have to offer You is my anger. So here it is. I put it in Your hand.

◇◇◇

Loving Father, I feel as though being so angry with You has separated me from You. Remind me that that's a lie. Nothing can separate me from Your love—not even my anger.

◇◇◇

Jesus, as I say with You, "My God, my God, why have you forsaken me?" (Matthew 27:46 NIV)—may I also be able to pray, "Father, into your hands I commit my spirit" (Luke 23:46 NIV).

Lord Jesus, I have to confess that I feel angry with You. Why are You doing this to my family? Why won't You take this away from us? And Lord—thank You that You are big enough to handle my anger.

◇◇◇

God, You are all-knowing. You love me completely, and You know what's best for me. You will never leave me, and You will meet each and every need I have— even if You do it in ways I don't expect.

◇◇◇

There is so much anger and confusion inside me, Jesus. I don't know what to think. I can't focus on anything. Please heal me. Strengthen me for whatever comes next.

◇◇◇

God, I know You are all-powerful. You are strong enough to deal with my anger. You can get me through this.

◇◇◇

In the end, God, You have not destined me for anger but to obtain salvation through my Lord Jesus Christ, who died for me so that whether I am awake or asleep, alive in this world or in the next world, I might live with Him. Therefore, help me to encourage my friends and family, who are also struggling now. May we build up one another. (1 Thessalonians 5:9–11)

◇◇◇

Loving God, I've noticed that I'm more likely to get angry when I'm focused on myself. I want to be in control—and when I'm not, even little things upset me. Remind me that You are in control, not me. My life is in Your hands. I don't need to feel frustrated when things don't go the way I want. Instead, I can wait to see what new thing You will do.

Jesus, why do I get so angry with others when they don't act the way I want? My own behavior is far from perfect. Replace my frustration and resentment with humility and patience, I pray.

◇◇◇

Lord, teach me to follow James's advice (1:19–20): Help me to be quick to listen to what others have to say; slow to speak; and even slower to lose my temper. My anger will never produce Your righteousness in my life.

◇◇◇

Remind me, God, that You are the giver of all good gifts. You don't withhold any good gift from Your children whom You love. Sometimes I feel like You're not giving me what I want or need. I grow angry with You even though I feel terribly guilty about that anger. Please forgive me and show me how to trust You even when I'm not getting my way.

◇◇◇

God, I often lose control and act in ways that I wish I didn't. It keeps happening. Please guard my heart and my tongue. . .and please, Lord, help me to have self-control. I long to be more like Jesus.

◇◇◇

Father, Your Word says, "Good sense makes one slow to anger, and it is his glory to overlook an offense" (Proverbs 19:11 ESV). I need to consider what it's like to be on the other side of me, especially when I get angry. I don't respond well when people get angry with me; why would they respond to my anger any differently? I can assert myself and make the points I need to make without losing my temper, but I need Your help to increase my self-awareness and to respond humbly.

God, it occurs to me that my anger is really an expression of pride. I thought I was setting someone straight, but I was really just putting myself in Your place. Forgive me. Only You know the whole story behind every situation. Only You know the full motives in each person's heart, including mine. I want to put others ahead of myself and their interests ahead of mine.

◇◇◇

Heavenly Father, I sometimes hurt my spouse and children when I'm angry. I hurt them with my words. I say things that I know are unkind, and later, I feel so guilty for it. Reveal to me where this anger comes from, God. Show me the hurt within my heart that reacts with a hot temper. Root out the bitterness in me. I am ready to get to work. I want this to change.

◇◇◇

God, You want Your children to live at peace with one another. You tell us never to let the sun go down on our anger. I find myself stewing about a situation when I go to sleep and then picking up right where I left off the next day as soon as I wake. I know this is not Your will for me. Help me to value my relationships more and to resolve conflicts quickly.

◇◇◇

Father, I come from a long line of angry ancestors. I know what it is to go without kind words or physical affection. I've lived for so long without my father's blessing, and it has made me bitter and prone to angry words and actions. Give me Your blessing, Father, so that I can break this cycle and love my kids the way I should have been loved—the way You love me. May I teach them to love You and Your Word.

Remind me not to shove and push and quarrel with others,
trying to get what I want—and let me instead simply turn to You
to satisfy my desires, trusting You will give me whatever I truly
need. Strip away my anger, Lord. Let me clothe myself
instead with love and self-control.

◇◇◇

Help me not to sin in my anger, Father. Everyone feels angry
sometimes. I never want to act on it. Help me to take
a deep breath and first come to You in prayer.
Rescue me from my own anger, I pray.

◇◇◇

Jesus, I try to get rid of my anger, but it keeps coming back.
Show me the source of my anger. Is it because I am hurt? Or
afraid? Is some reaction from my childhood being triggered?
Am I jealous and insecure? Am I unsure of my own worth in this
situation? Reveal the truth to me, whatever it is—and then heal
me, I pray. Only then will I be able to truly turn from anger.

◇◇◇

God, remind me that the sun should not go down on my anger.
Help me not to go to bed nursing a grudge that will haunt
my sleep and get up with me in the morning. Instead, let me
value my relationships enough that I commit myself to
working through the conflicts that arise. I know
You want us to live in harmony.

ANXIETY

Don't fret or worry. Instead of worrying, pray. Let petitions and praises shape your worries into prayers, letting God know your concerns. Before you know it, a sense of God's wholeness, everything coming together for good, will come and settle you down. It's wonderful what happens when Christ displaces worry at the center of your life.

PHILIPPIANS 4:6–7 MSG

It's easy to be anxious. Are our loved ones safe? Will we have enough money for what we need? Will we do a good job on a challenging responsibility that's coming up? Will our friends accept us? Will we be able to get everything done that needs doing? Will the people we love most make wise decisions? Anxieties pile up around us, everywhere we turn.

We need to learn to transform our anxiety into a prayer. Each time we find ourselves fretting over what will happen regarding some situation, we can turn over that specific set of circumstances to God. As we make this practice a habit, we will find our trust in God is growing. Instead of anxiety, Christ will dwell at the center of our lives.

I'm underwater, Lord, pressed down by weights I can't lift.
All I want is to know what You want me to do, but it feels like
I'm running out of air. I'm spending a lot of energy trying not
to panic, and it's making me physically sick. Hear me,
please—I need air! Give me Your Spirit now
and help me to breathe again.

◇◇◇

Lord, I'm a worrier. I worry about my family and my friends.
I worry about the future because there are so many unknowns.
I know that in my anxiety I sin because I'm not trusting You.
Please replace my fear with faith. Please help me to rely
on You when I begin to worry needlessly.

◇◇◇

When I'm anxious, I pray that You will remind me that I must
cast my cares on You, Jesus. You ask me to do this. You tell
me to cast them. That means rid myself of them.
That means throw them with all my might at Your
feet. Help me to truly surrender to You, Lord.

◇◇◇

God, no one knows the secret fears that I carry around in
my heart. No one but You. May I lay down fear and pick up
confidence instead. You are my confidence and my peace.

◇◇◇

I know, Lord Jesus, that I must trust You with my children.
I feel so responsible for them! They are young and vulnerable.
They may make the wrong choices. Help me to trust You with
my most precious gifts. You made them and know them far
better than even I do. Be with them, Lord, and watch over
them. Cause me to trust that You have them in Your care.

Why do I surrender my peace? Help me to hope in You,
knowing that soon I will be praising You for all You have
done. You are the one who will make me smile
again. You are my God. (Psalm 43:5)

◇◇◇

Lord, help me stop feeling so anxious but instead, in every
situation, with thanksgiving, remind me to turn to You in
prayer. Thank You that Your peace, which goes beyond
all understanding, will guard my heart and mind
in Christ Jesus. (Philippians 4:6–7)

◇◇◇

Because I dwell in the secret place of the Most High, Lord,
I shall abide under the shadow of the Almighty. You are my
refuge and my fortress, my God. In You I will trust. You have
delivered me from all of life's snares and dangers. You have
covered me with Your feathers, and under Your wings I
take refuge. Your truth is my shield. (Psalm 91:1–4)

◇◇◇

I do not need to worry in the night, Lord, nor do I need to fret
about dangers during the day. Neither sickness nor destruction
are my concern. Even though people all around me are in
trouble, I still don't need to worry, because You are my refuge.
You—the Most High—are my dwelling place. You have given
Your angels the job of looking after me. No matter what dangers
I face, I am safe. Because of Your love, You will deliver me.
You will set me in a high place. When I call on You, You answer
me. If trouble comes, You will still be with me. You will deliver
me and honor me. You will show me Your salvation all
through my life. So why should I worry? (Psalm 91:5–16)

Lord, You are in complete control—and You are greater than any of my worries. I cannot change the future; I cannot change the circumstances of my life—so worrying is simply a waste of time and energy! Teach me that my energy could be better spent in prayer.

◇◇◇

Thank You, Father, for giving me the confidence that You are for me and with me. I know that life holds nothing that You can't overcome. No power is greater than You. I can rest in Your arms today, knowing that You have everything under control.

◇◇◇

Jesus, You know that I often have Martha's focus on life: I'm anxious and harried, anxious about the many details of my life. Give me instead Mary's heart. Help me to always choose Your presence as my first priority—and then my heart will be at peace.

◇◇◇

God, this anxiety is wearing me down. It's a spiritual battle, but it's even taking a physical toll on me. I can't sleep or eat properly. I'm exhausted. Heal my mind and heart. Take away the fear and the panic. Replace them with peace and calm. I long to rest in You. I know that I can't do it on my own.

◇◇◇

Anxiety is like a prison that I cannot break free from no matter how hard I try. I need help, God. It is so hard to admit that. Give me wisdom this day about how to get help. Strip away my pride.

◇◇◇

Use my anxiety, Lord, to remind me that I'm dependent on Your love. Let each nagging fear be a nudge that turns me toward You and Your strength.

God, You know my every anxiety. I cast each one
on You, for I know You care for me.

◇◇◇

You are a good, good Father, and I am loved by You.
When I'm afraid of others or of circumstances, remind me
of Your goodness. When I feel I cannot face the future,
remind me that I am Your beloved child. You are always
good, and I am always loved. I am going to be just fine.

◇◇◇

God, I notice that when I pray regularly, my anxiety decreases.
I trust in You. Strengthen my prayer life that I might
be freed from these anxious thoughts.

◇◇◇

Father, I am stressed out. Remind me that I am not alone in
my struggles. You are my Shepherd, my light and salvation,
my rock, and my refuge.

◇◇◇

I realize, Father, that I'm more likely to be anxious when
I'm focused on the wrong things. Help me to lay up my
treasures in You rather accumulating things in this world.
I need have no worries about eternal treasures!

◇◇◇

Help me, Jesus, to follow the example of the birds and
flowers, who never fret. You never forget to nourish them.
Remind me that I am even more precious in Your sight.

The cost of anxiety is too high, Lord. It uses up my energy.
It takes its toll on my body, giving me headaches and stomach
problems. Even my immune system suffers. And meanwhile,
worrying about tomorrow robs me of today's joy. Lord,
I don't want to pay the cost of anxiety any longer.
Take my worries from me, I pray. Let me trust in You.

◇◇◇

God, I am trusting that praying will bring me peace. You said
I shouldn't be anxious—about anything!—but instead, I should
bring all my requests to You and thank You for all You've done.
I'm counting on Your promise that when I do that, "the peace
of God, which transcends all understanding, will guard your
hearts and your minds in Christ Jesus" (Philippians 4:7 NIV).
Thank You, God, for caring about the things I care about.

◇◇◇

Anxiety paralyzes me, God. Please set me free. Allow me to take
whatever action needs to be taken—and trust the rest to You.

◇◇◇

Teach me, Loving Creator, to trust You with all my heart. Help
me not to depend on my own understanding. I know that when
I seek Your guidance instead, You will lead me on straight paths.
I don't want to rely on my own wisdom. Instead, I choose to
respect Your Word; I will stay away from anything that pulls me
from You. When I do all this, my heart will be at peace—and
anxiety will no longer steal my body's health (Proverbs 3).

◇◇◇

I'm holding onto my faith, but it feels like a fistful of sand.
Don't let me slip through Your grasp today, Father.
Guard my heart and mind with Your peace, grace,
and love. I trust You. I trust You. I trust You.

ARGUMENTS

Again I say, don't get involved in foolish, ignorant arguments that only start fights. A servant of the Lord must not quarrel but must be kind to everyone.
2 TIMOTHY 2:23–24 NLT

No matter how hard we try, sooner or later we seem to end up in an argument with someone—and most of the time, it's someone close to us. Coworkers, neighbors, friends, family members, spouses—those are the people with whom we're most likely to argue. Small differences of opinion lead to hurt feelings. The hostilities escalate. Eventually, we may not even remember what started it all. All we know is that we're locked in an argument, and neither side wants to be the first to give in and apologize.

But God doesn't want us to quarrel. He calls us instead to kindness. This may mean setting our own opinions aside as being not all that important. . .so that instead we can hear what another thinks. It may mean letting go of our own choices. . .so we can make room for another to choose. It may require that we keep our mouth shut when angry words threaten to burst out of us. . . so that someone else has a chance to speak.

Does it (whatever "it" is) really matter all that much? Or can we choose to make kindness matter far more?

Lord, I'm in conflict with someone, and my anger and frustration are building. I need Your perspective on this situation. Help me to do what's right in Your eyes.

◇◇◇

Lord, I know You really don't care how eloquently I present my case; if I don't speak in love, I am like a noisy gong or a clanging cymbal. The love You call me to is patient and kind; it's not arrogant or rude, it doesn't envy or boast, it doesn't insist on its own way, and it's not irritable or resentful (1 Corinthians 13:1–6). Teach me to stop arguing—and instead simply love.

◇◇◇

God, Your Word emphasizes love over and over again. In 1 Corinthians, we read that it's even greater than hope and peace. Please help me to show love to others. I don't want to have an argumentative spirit. Please help me to be kind and loving at all times, even when things don't go my way.

◇◇◇

Remind me, Father, that I may be the only Jesus some will ever see. Please help me to be a loving example of what it means to be a Christian.

◇◇◇

When I am tempted to argue, remind me to remain silent. There is a time for everything (Ecclesiastes 3), including a time to speak and a time to be quiet.

◇◇◇

Sometimes, Jesus, I think I'm arguing on Your behalf. Remind me that You don't need my help convincing others to believe in You. That's Your Spirit's job. My job is to simply carry Your love out into the world.

Lord, I know that the tongue can be a positive or a negative. Help me to use my words to bring You honor and glory rather than cause petty arguments. You take no pleasure in hearing Your children squabble with one another over issues that really don't matter in the long run. Help me to be more like Jesus. Help me to be slow to anger.

◇◇◇

I want to bear fruit for You in this world, Father. I know that without spending time in prayer daily, I lose sight of my purpose on earth. I'm to bring glory to You and to lead others to know You as their personal Savior. How can I do this if I'm constantly at odds with those around me? Help me to love those whom You have placed in my circles of influence. I want to be known as a peacemaker.

◇◇◇

I need to figure out this whole *need vs. want* thing. I want to honor You by seeking what others need above what I want. I don't have to argue to get what I want; I just need to trust You and You will provide.

◇◇◇

Proverbs warns against stirring up anger. It says that this will bring nothing but trouble. Please help me to have the strength to walk away from arguments, Lord. I'm imperfect, and I will fail at this sometimes. Give me then the wisdom and patience to deal with the outcome. Give me the humility to be the first to apologize and to make amends.

I know that You don't want me to covet what others have
(Exodus 20:17). Jealousy stirs up anger and arguing among
even Christian brothers and sisters. Help me to celebrate with
others when good things come to them rather than grow
jealous or bitter toward them. I want my heart to
be right before You and before men.

◇◇◇

Creator God, use my voice and words to carry Your Spirit's
presence into every conversation. Let me practice soft
answers that calm tempers, while I avoid harsh
words that stir up anger (Proverbs 15:1).

◇◇◇

May I use my conversations only for Your glory, Lord.
Remind me to seek to bless others with each thing I say.
If arguments and cross words pour out of me, how can
I claim to be filled with Your Spirit? Cleanse my heart
first, dear God, and then my mouth and all its words,
so that my life is not filled with contradiction.

◇◇◇

Give me strength, loving Lord, to let go of what I think—
and instead pursue only that which will help build peace,
that which will encourage, that which will please You.

◇◇◇

Father, I'm trying to think of a time when I won someone over
by using angry, harsh words during an argument. And I can't.
I may have made my point, but I lost trust—and a chance to
honor You. Forgive me for all the times I've tried to defend
myself or You unnecessarily, or put a principle ahead of a
person, or righteousness ahead of relationship. Let my
offenses be limited as I stick to the truth of the Gospel.

Lord, I need to bear in mind that it isn't my job but the Holy Spirit's to convict people of sin (John 16:8). Yes, the world is broken and full of sinners. Yes, Your righteous standard condemns all of us, and yes, the world will be judged. But I can know all of this and not let it lead to condemning, judgmental words. I came to Christ because Your Spirit did His work in me. When it comes to my words, remind me to give Him space to work in others' hearts too. Then I can stand for Your truth in a gracious and loving way, and maybe the Spirit will work through me instead of despite me.

◇◇◇

The book of Proverbs tells me, Lord, that if I churn milk, I'll get butter. . .if I hit someone in the nose, it will bleed. . . and if I stir up anger, I will get into trouble (30:33). Help me to walk away from arguments! And when I fail to do so, give me wisdom, patience, courage, and love to deal with the consequences.

◇◇◇

God, my mind is swimming with all the points I want to make, with what I think this other person needs to hear. But it's all mixed up with my anger and frustration, and possibly my self-righteousness and judgmental thinking. Give me clarity and the ability to think before I speak. If I need to take some time to sort it out, help me to find solutions, not comebacks or ways to embarrass others. If it turns out there's a real issue, help me to address it in a direct and respectful way—to deal with the issue and not attack the person. Fill me with Your Spirit so I can represent You well.

BANKRUPTCY

And my God will meet all your needs according to the riches of his glory in Christ Jesus.
PHILIPPIANS 4:19 NIV

We all know that we are to put our trust in God rather than money. Even our currency reminds us that "in God we trust." In the world where we live, it makes no sense to put our trust in the economy, our jobs, or our bank accounts. And yet, over and over we forget. We start to depend on finances for our security.

And then the economy crashes, we're laid off, and our bank account dwindles. Maybe we make stupid mistakes along the way. We may never have thought we'd ever be facing bankruptcy—and yet here it is, staring us in the face. It can be a terrifying moment!

Even now, however, God is unchanged. He is *still* able to meet all our needs from the unending wealth of His great riches! The Creator of the universe is on our side. He will take care of us, no matter what.

Our money never gave us security in the first place. Only God truly keeps us safe.

Jesus, when I received You as Lord and Savior, You gave me a fresh start, a chance to break from my past and be the person You made me to be. Now that I've reached a point where I've decided that declaring bankruptcy is my best financial option, I ask You to give me a fresh start here too. Help me to put lessons I've learned into practice so that I never have to put myself and my family through this again.

◇◇◇

Heavenly Father, my personal storehouses are utterly empty. My finances are a desert. I am looking to You. Open Your hand and give whatever it is I most need. I trust You to know what that is. Send Your rain to water my life.

◇◇◇

Lord, remind me of what is most important. It would be easy to pray that You would restore my finances, but instead I pray for courage, self-confidence, and humility: the courage, self-confidence, and humility to start over again.

◇◇◇

Lord, I know I need to pay off my debts, and I know I've failed to do so. Some of this has been due to circumstances beyond my control, but when I've gotten desperate, I've tried to handle it myself—and gotten nowhere. I'm giving all of this over to You, God. You can make a way where there is no other. Lead me and teach me.

◇◇◇

Remind me, Lord, that others' situations are far worse than mine. You have blessed me in so many ways. Help me to focus on those blessings now, during this time of financial trouble, and make me a blessing to others.

Lord, I've made mistakes before. I don't want to make them again. Send me wise financial counselors. May I know whom to listen to. Show me the way forward.

◇◇◇

I'm relying on You, Creator God. I'm done with trusting my own plans. Direct my steps, I pray. Let me trust in You.

◇◇◇

Father, in Proverbs it says that wisdom, understanding, and knowledge are necessary to financial success (24:3–4). Dear Lord, build my financial house with wisdom, establish it with understanding, and fill all its rooms with the riches of knowledge. Restore my finances in Your timing, I pray.

◇◇◇

Bankruptcy isn't the problem; my attitude is. Guide me as I seek to learn about handling money in a way that honors You, and protect me and my family as we sort this out.

◇◇◇

Jesus, let me not be so preoccupied with my own financial problems that I forget that others are in need. You told us in Your Word that it is more blessed to give than to receive, so may I never forget to give. Let me be generous with my time and energy; show me ways I can reach out and be of use to others.

◇◇◇

I ask You for mercy, Father. The burden is crushing me, affecting my health and my relationships. I confess it's because I've tried to do things my way instead of Yours. Be with me and help me to make it right, to pursue bankruptcy only when I've exhausted all other options, and to heal the relationships with family and friends I've hurt.

BARGAINING WITH GOD

"Far be it from you to do such a thing. . . .
Will not the Judge of all the earth do right?"
GENESIS 18:25 NIV

Psychologists recognize bargaining as another way that we come to terms with a new and frightening reality. When we pray, "Dear God, if You'll only make this go away, I'll do this. . . ," we are being completely normal. And we're not alone; even the great heroes of the Bible tried to bargain with God.

Bargaining doesn't change reality. But God understands, and He listens. We can be confident enough in His love that we dare to say to Him whatever we feel. We can even say, "God, don't do this! Why would You let this happen? You know it's not right—so make it go away!" We don't need to hesitate to come to God with whatever is in our hearts.

How can I bear this, God? It's too much. I can't do it.
Please, God, please don't make me face this.

◇◇◇

Draw near to me, my loving Lord. Be with me as I twist and
turn, trying to escape this diagnosis. Touch me. Hold me steady.
Stand between me and whatever lies ahead.

◇◇◇

Dear Jesus, I am throwing myself on You. I'm pleading with You
to send Your healing, as You did with the crowds who followed
You when You walked this earth. I know I don't need
to persuade You to love me more than You already do. I don't
have to bribe You to have my best interests always in mind.
Your loving-kindness is already with me, each step of the way.

BETRAYAL

It is not an enemy who taunts me—I could bear that. It is not my foes who so arrogantly insult me—I could have hidden from them. Instead, it is you— my equal, my companion and close friend. What good fellowship we once enjoyed as we walked together to the house of God.
PSALM 55:12–14 NLT

Sooner or later, all of us feel betrayed in one way or another by someone we've trusted. People let us down. Sometimes it's unintentional, and that hurts badly enough. It's even worse when a friend purposefully stabs us in the back. The hurt can be overwhelming. We can't understand why anyone would treat us like that. It's easy to feel angry. It's only natural to want to put up our guard and protect ourselves against further pain.

It's far more challenging to follow Christ's example. He too knew what it was like to be betrayed by a friend. And yet He never rose His hand in anger, never spoke sharp words, never sought to return the blow in any way.

If we have chosen to be followers of Jesus Christ, then we too must find ways to respond with love to those who have hurt us.

Lord God, even though I want to strike back at my betrayer, I'm going to cry out to You instead. Your Word says, "Don't repay evil for evil. Don't retaliate with insults when people insult you. Instead, pay them back with a blessing. That is what God has called you to do, and he will grant you his blessing" (1 Peter 3:9 NLT). I can't do that without You though, so I give You my anger and my fear. Fill me with Your Spirit so I can turn my cheek and honor You.

◇◇◇

Heavenly Father, I feel so deeply hurt. I trusted this person. And I was betrayed. I know You tell me to guard my heart for it is the wellspring from which life flows. I didn't. I let my heart go too easily. I put it in the hands of another. In doing so, I was unfaithful to You, Lord. Hold me close. It hurts to find out this is not the person I thought I knew.

◇◇◇

Lord, it hurts to have a fickle friend. Even small betrayals leave wounds. I make plans with this friend who continues to break them at the last minute. Doesn't show up. Calls to cancel. Please guide me as to whether I should continue to show grace or perhaps back away a bit from this person. I need friends whom I can count on to be there.

◇◇◇

Jesus, even though I've been wronged, I want to respond like You did when You were wronged. You are my example: You committed no sin, and no deceit was found in Your mouth. When men hurled insults at You, You didn't retaliate. When You suffered, You made no threats. Instead You entrusted Yourself to Him who judges justly (1 Peter 2:22–23 NIV). You are my Lord and my Savior, and even though I feel the ache of betrayal in my gut, I choose to be like You.

Lord, I betrayed my friend. I shared information that was not to be shared. I have not been trustworthy. Whether my friend knows or not doesn't matter. I feel so guilty inside. Please forgive me for being a gossip. In the moment, it feels good to be the one in the know. Afterward, it saddens me that I was not true to my friend. "A gossip betrays a confidence, but a trustworthy person keeps a secret" (Proverbs 11:13 NIV).

◇◇◇

None of the disciples wanted to believe that he could be the one who would betray You. And yet, in reality, it could have been any of them—just as it could be me. We are all sinners. We fall short. We mess up. Judas betrayed You, Jesus. It hurts me to read the story. Please keep my heart true to You, no matter the cost, all the days of my life.

◇◇◇

Dear Father, help me to forgive those who have trespassed the boundaries of my life—as You have forgiven my trespasses. Give me strength to forgive the debts which brought me hurt—as You have forgiven all my debts. Remind me that I too have made mistakes. I have hurt and betrayed others, and worst of all, I have betrayed You.

◇◇◇

Lord, make me strong in Your might. Help me to put on Your entire armor, so that I can resist the devil's schemes. I know that ultimately, this is a spiritual situation. I'm not dealing with flesh and blood who want to hurt me, but rather the spiritual forces of evil. Let me clasp the shield of faith, so that I can stand firm, even now. Armor me in truth and righteousness. (Ephesians 6:10–16)

I sit here hurting in disbelief. Betrayal stings. You know the sting of betrayal. You were betrayed by Peter three times before the cock crowed. He said he would never turn away from You and yet, it happened. Remind me that in our humanity we are weak. Give me a forgiving spirit that I might reach a place where I can forgive those who have betrayed me.

◇◇◇

God, it seems like marriage is a thing of the past. I watch my friends' marriages disintegrating. Help me to remain true to my wedding vows and loyal to my mate.

◇◇◇

Father, I don't think of myself as someone who has enemies. But it turns out I do—and it's someone I know and trusted. I'm hurt and angry. But I also realize You're giving me a chance to do something You did—love my enemy— and that You're also giving me a chance to live without bitterness and grudge-holding.

◇◇◇

Give ear to my prayer, Lord God, and don't hide Yourself from my pleas for mercy! Listen to me and answer me. I hear the voices of my enemies, I feel their oppression, and I am filled with restlessness and pain. They have a grudge against me, and now they're heaping trouble on me. My heart is anguished. I'm overcome with fear. How I wish I had wings like a dove and could fly away from all this! I would fly somewhere safe, somewhere I could be alone without having to deal with any of this. (Psalm 55:1–7)

Father, even as the sting of betrayal pulses inside me,
I remember that I'm a citizen of a different realm—Your
kingdom. As much as my flesh is pushing me to dish up revenge,
to plot the downfall of my betrayer, I hold to the truth that
because I'm Yours, I don't have to respond with vengeance. In
fact, You have a better (though harder) way for me: "Don't hit
back; discover beauty in everyone. If you've got it in you,
get along with everybody. Don't insist on getting even; that's not
for you to do. 'I'll do the judging,' says God. 'I'll take care of it' "
(Romans 12:17–19 MSG). Hold me up, Father, and protect me.
Remember that I chose You at this low moment and lift me up.

◇◇◇

Jesus, I know You understand how I feel. You, too, were betrayed
by one of Your closest friends. And just as I would never focus
on Judas's role in the story rather than Yours, I choose now
to look to You, rather than the people who have let me down.
You're the One I'm following. That hasn't changed.

◇◇◇

Lord, I can't believe that someone would turn on me like this—
all for the sake of climbing the ladder or getting the credit!
Please use this to teach me how it feels to be betrayed
that I might never treat others in such a manner.

◇◇◇

Use my pain at this betrayal for Your purposes, Creator God.
Teach me through it. Draw me closer to You.
Deepen my compassion for others.

BITERNESS

Get rid of all bitterness, rage and anger, brawling and slander, along with every form of malice. Be kind and compassionate to one another, forgiving each other, just as in Christ God forgave you.

EPHESIANS 4:31–32 NIV

Any good gardener knows that it's just as important to get the weeds out as it is to plant the seeds. Certainly nothing healthy or beautiful can grow in a garden full of weeds. Bitterness, anger, and gossip are a lot like weeds. They start small, but soon, if they are not watched closely, they completely take over. Just as you wouldn't allow weeds to steal the nutrients of your garden's soil and suffocate new life, be on guard against this happening in your heart.

When you sense a hint of bitterness, trample it out. Ask God to pluck it from your heart so that it doesn't have the opportunity to gain control. Think about the grace that Jesus has shown to you and determine in your heart to demonstrate grace to those around you, even those who may receive unfair advantages or who may have hurt you in some way. Replace bitterness with kindness and forgiveness. This is God's will for you in Christ Jesus.

Lord, it's hard not to compare others' lives with my own.
I see another's nice things. I'm envious of another's spouse
who seems to be more caring than my own. I watch another's
children succeeding in areas where my own are struggling.
Remind me that it's not good to compare myself to
others. Help me to have a thankful and content
heart that is right before You.

◇◇◇

God, You name some things in Your Word that I should not
allow to be part of my life. You tell me, in fact, to "get rid of"
them. Bitterness is on Your list. Like an earthly father who does
not allow his child to consume spoiled food because it will
cause sickness, You warn me against bitterness. You know
it has the potential to ruin my life.

◇◇◇

Lord, I'm bitter about a situation. You know all the players and
the plot of the story. You know the details before I even spill
them out before You. Please calm my spirit and give me the
ability to let it go. I'm hurting myself more than anyone else
when I hold on to this and stew about it day and night.

◇◇◇

Heavenly Father, I know that bitterness can take root and grow
like a wild ivy, spreading through my very being. Please help
me to be aware of its presence and root it out quickly.

Jesus, someone did me wrong. You saw it. You were there. Why shouldn't I hold a grudge? I've been hurt and mistreated. You understand, You say? You too were wronged. You were treated unjustly. Your heart did not grow hard even when the soldiers put bitter vinegar to Your parched lips as You hung dying on the cross. You asked the Father to forgive them. Grant me just a tiny bit of that strength, Savior, that I might forgive those who have acted unfairly toward me.

◇◇◇

Help me to focus on blessings over betrayals and friends over foes. Lord, I thank You for the people in my life, the opportunities You have given me, and the needs You meet every single day. I will choose to focus on the good rather than allow bitterness to fester in my heart.

◇◇◇

One day at a time, Lord. Help me to forgive and forget and to simply take one day at a time. Help me to remember that nothing touches my life if it has not first been filtered through Your fingers. If You have allowed me to walk through a trial, there is a reason for it. Please keep me from becoming bitter toward You, my loving and faithful God.

◆◆◆◆◆◆◆
CHALLENGES

When you go to war against your enemies and see horses and chariots and an army greater than yours, do not be afraid of them, because the LORD your God, who brought you up out of Egypt, will be with you. When you are about to go into battle, the priest shall come forward and address the army. He shall say: "Hear, Israel: Today you are going into battle against your enemies. Do not be fainthearted or afraid; do not panic or be terrified by them. For the LORD your God is the one who goes with you to fight for you against your enemies to give you victory."

DEUTERONOMY 20:1–4 NIV

◆

We're not likely to ever face an army of horses and chariots—but some days, the challenges in our lives can seem just as threatening as any battlefield. When that happens, we need to follow the advice given here in Deuteronomy. First, remember all that God has done for us in the past. Second, believe that He is the One who will fight our battles, not us. We can rely on Him for the victory.

Lord, I want to see this obstacle through Your eyes, to trust that Your purposes are in it. Your Word says that the testing of my faith produces patience and that when I'm not sure what to do, I should ask You for wisdom and You'll give it to me (James 1:2–5). I want to jump in and fix this situation myself, but I admit that I don't know enough right now to act. Show me how and when to get involved, and remind me to seek Your purposes in this.

◇◇◇

Be my strong tower, Lord. In the midst of all my life's challenges, I run to You. Keep me safe.

◇◇◇

Just as Noah built an ark and gathered pairs of animals when there was not a rain cloud in sight, I will face this day in complete faith that You are who You say You are. You are the God of the universe, and You are on my side. Help me know what to do regarding this obstacle that's in my way.

◇◇◇

I think about young David with his slingshot. He was able to kill the giant not because of his own strength or expertise but because his confidence was in You, God. He was fighting the right battle. He was on the right side. Draw me close to You. I don't want to be on the front lines in this battle without You at my side as my commanding officer.

◇◇◇

You are my refuge and strength, God, my ever-present help in the midst of challenges. Therefore, I won't be scared—even if the earth gives way beneath my feet, even if the mountains fall into the oceans (Psalm 46:1–3). In the midst of all these challenges, I know You are with me.

I tend to grow closer to You during times of trials. When life is
just moving along normally, I often drift from You. When I face
a challenge, I run to Your side. I'm more faithful in prayer.
I seek You in Your Word, and I walk closer to Your
side. Challenges can really be a positive thing in my life!

◇◇◇

God, I'm struggling as a Christian in a very worldly society.
I feel like others don't understand why I make the choices I
make. It's hard being different. Your Word promises that the
more I participate in the sufferings of Christ, the greater joy I
will experience one day when His glory is fully revealed (1 Peter
4:13). Give me the endurance I need to stand firm in my faith.

◇◇◇

I have set You always before me, Lord. I'm looking only at
You. And because You're there, right beside me,
no challenge can shake me (Psalm 16:8).

◇◇◇

God, I feel overwhelmed. This problem is too big for me,
and I need Your help. I know that nothing happens
without You knowing, so let that be enough for me.
You are my strength and my peace.

◇◇◇

Heavenly Father, the challenges I face are not unique to me.
There's nothing strange about facing trials and hardships.
Believers have walked through rough situations for generations.
I should not be shocked when a challenge comes my way (1 Peter
4:12). Just as You have stood with Christ-followers of the past,
stand with me now, I pray. Walk with me, Lord. Carry me.

"Joshua fought the battle of Jericho, and the walls came tumbling down." I remember singing the song as a child, Lord. I was so surprised that when the men blew the trumpets and broke the pitchers, they were successful. Who would have ever thought? I could use some walls to come tumbling down about now, God. Show me the way. Make me open to unorthodox methods. I will tackle this challenge in any way You lead me, and then I will be able to stand back and watch You work. Thank You in advance for the guidance I know You will provide.

◇◇◇

Father, I confess that when I'm facing a trial, my tendency is to ask why You've let it happen instead of what You're doing in me by allowing it. I trust that You are sovereign, that You are good, and that You will strengthen my faith through this challenge if I'm open to You. I set aside my desire to know all the reasons why, and instead I choose to trust that Your grace is sufficient for me.

◇◇◇

Teach me about You, God, here in the midst of this situation. May I learn more about Your power, Your love, and Your amazing creativity. I know there's nothing too hard for You!

◇◇◇

You are the Lord of the Universe. You created worlds from nothing. You formed me within my mother's womb and brought me into being. You have been with me, in every challenge I have ever faced, since I was born. With each new test, I've grown. You've revealed Yourself in new ways all through my life. I'm waiting now to see what You will do next!

God, my fear is threatening to cut me off from You. I'm afraid of failing to overcome this obstacle, of missing Your purposes in it, of letting others down. I confess my fear; help my unbelief. You are my Rock and my Salvation. Even if the earth crumbles beneath me, I know You are with me. I will look forward to seeing what You accomplish in and through me as I face this.

◇◇◇

Lord God, I confess that I was getting all fired up about taking on this challenge but failed to seek You. I know Your Word warns against boasting about tomorrow (James 4:13–16). I know enough of Your grace, mercy, and oversight that I should know better than to make plans without You. Thank You for prompting me by Your Spirit to seek You now. I ask for Your guidance and blessing on the challenge in front of me. Help me to achieve Your will as I face it.

◇◇◇

The challenge that lies ahead, Lord, is too big for me. My self-confidence fails. I can't help but compare how big the challenge is to my meager abilities for confronting it. My faith wavers. But I know that when I admit how weak I truly am, then You have the chance to reveal Your strength. The challenge that lies ahead shrinks when I compare it to the immensity of You. And I finally realize that my perception of the challenges that lie ahead all depends on my perspective. Keep me focused on You and Your power.

◇◇◇

Jesus, I believe I can do all things—
because You make me strong (Philippians 4:13).

CHRONIC ILLNESS

*Have mercy on me, O Lord, for I am weak;
O Lord, heal me, for my bones are troubled.*
PSALM 6:2 NKJV

When we face a chronic illness, we often feel a spectrum of emotions: anger, despair, embarrassment, apathy, depression, loneliness, confusion, fear, sorrow. We may feel it's just not fair. At the same time, we don't know what to expect next. We want to give up. We want to scream. We long for someone who understands. We wish we could run away. We're mad at God. We want to hide away and never get out of bed. We long for our old lives back.

All these feelings are normal. They do not make us less of a Christian. They do not interfere with our relationship with God, so long as we share them with Him. We will need help coping with this condition—doctors, counselors, friends, family—but most of all, we will need to find God even here, in the midst of our illness. When we see His face, then we can begin to move forward once more.

Jesus, I realize that this sickness is part of what You came to redeem. You've made me a new person spiritually, and I know that when You return, You'll make me a new person physically as well. In the meantime though, I'm sick, and it's not going away. And while I don't like it, I want to sit still and let You work. Father, I know that even as my body fails, I can become more like Jesus in seeking Your will, drinking from the cup You've given me, and trusting You to redeem this suffering.

◇◇◇

Lord God, give me eyes to see You work through my illness. You have plans that go beyond my pain—plans for my family and friends, plans for my doctors and caregivers, plans to let me minister to those who are suffering the way I am. I hate being sick, but I love You for giving me a reason to hope and to endure with expectation. I'm waiting, Lord; make something good come out of this.

◇◇◇

I am sick, Lord—and yet I choose to bless Your name. I feel diminished by this illness—and yet I give You all that I have left to offer. Heal me, Lord, if it be Your will. Redeem my life from destruction. Crown me with Your loving-kindness and tender mercies (Psalm 103:1–4).

◇◇◇

Jesus, You healed the sick. You caused the lame to walk. You took away the lepers' spots. I don't understand why You won't heal me in the same way. I know that there are things we just won't understand until we get to heaven. Please comfort me as I wait to understand Your ways.

Heavenly Father, this illness has begun to define me.
I want my identity to be in Jesus Christ and not in my sickness.
Please remind me that I am a cherished heir of the King,
saved by grace through faith in the Messiah. I'm not just
a homebound sick person. I have value and worth
because I am part of the family of God.

◇◇◇

Merciful God, my life seems so dark. I don't know how to
rise above this illness. Be my sun, I pray. Rise over my life with
healing in Your wings. Release me from the walls of disease
that hold me captive. Allow me to run free, like a calf that
runs out of the barn when spring comes. (Malachi 4:2)

◇◇◇

Father, I am watching someone I love suffer, and it is so hard.
I've never felt so helpless, so unable to make a difference. Only
You can make something good come out of this. All I can say is,
"Here I am." If I can be of service, let me serve. If I can just be
there, let me be there. Even as I ask You to heal the one
I love, let me be Your hands and ears for them.

◇◇◇

Just as the apostle Paul prayed for You to remove the thorn from
his flesh, I pray for this thorn to be taken from my life. I wait in
expectation of what You will do. You will either remove it or You
will continue to walk with me through this adversity, using it to
strengthen my faith. I trust You, Lord, to do what is best for me.

I'm so tired of being sick. It keeps me from doing the things I long to do. I used to think nothing of running here and there. I wanted my life to slow down. Now I long to be busy again. Show me in some way today that I am not forgotten.

◇◇◇

Today I pray that each time I begin to dwell on what I *can't* do, Lord, You will bring to mind something that I *can.* I'm still able to do many things even though I'm ill. I can pray. I can encourage someone over the phone. I can do some things even though I'm not able to leave my home. Replace my negative thoughts with hopeful, positive ones. I can. I can. I can.

◇◇◇

Jesus, when You walked this earth, I know You healed all sorts of diseases. People were always reaching out to You, clamoring for Your healing. Just the touch of Your robe sent Your healing power flowing out to those who had been sick for years. Jesus, I believe You are the same now as You were then. You are filled with healing power. If I could only touch Your robe!

◇◇◇

I know, Lord, that You don't always choose to heal those who are ill. Sometimes instead, You ask sick people to bear their infirmity. And yet even then, I believe You bring healing, the deepest healing that reaches to the depths of a person's soul and lasts until eternity. God, I ask You for that kind of healing. You know I wish I could be free of this illness, here, now (right now!), in this life. But give me the strength to bear it, if instead, You will heal me in other ways, ways I need even more.

Father, let this sickness cultivate in me a wilderness mentality. Meet me in the midst of pain and side effects and endless appointments—all the points where my path intersects with others' paths—and let my belief in You color those interactions. There is so much more to this life than my pain. I want to see my hope—like when Job focused on seeing his Redeemer in person (Job 19:25). You sustain me today and every day, and You make the difficulties of my journey count for something greater—Your kingdom. Glorify Yourself in my broken body. I rest in the fact that, one day, You will glorify mine.

◇◇◇

God, teach me about prayer through this illness. I know You do not always choose to answer prayers as we might want. I know that our perspectives are often too limited for us to even understand what we truly need most. And yet I believe You always hear my prayers. You never ignore me. My prayers always connect me to You—and they open up a space where You can work in me. Please work in me, Lord. In whatever way You choose. This is my prayer.

◇◇◇

Teach me, God, to accept the reality of my life. I pray that one day I will be healed (whether in this life or the next)—but in the meantime, give me strength to work with what I have right now. Help me focus on all that I still have, rather than on my illness. Let me not shut away myself from others. May I still be useful to Your kingdom. Help my life to praise You.

CHRONIC PAIN

After you have suffered a little while, he will restore, support, and strengthen you, and he will place you on a firm foundation.
1 Peter 5:10 NLT

Life is full of pain. Even babies deal with colic and ear infections. As we get older, we experience backaches, headaches, stomachaches. Most of these come and go, but the older we get, the more pain seems to linger. Sometimes pain comes and stays forever.

When that happens, our entire lives may undergo a change. It's hard for us to interact with others the way we once did. We may no longer enjoy the activities we once liked best. Even our spiritual lives may suffer.

But God is with us even now. And He promises to restore, support, and strengthen us; so that even in the midst of pain, we will stand on a firm foundation.

Jesus, I know You suffered too. I know You are with me and that You will never leave me alone in my pain. Help me be more like You in the way I handle it.

◇◇◇

Jesus, I know You experienced pain. You did not hold Yourself separate from human experience, and You died on the cross in terrible agony. You understand what I'm feeling now. I can turn to You, knowing that even if no one else understands what I'm going through—You truly do understand.

◇◇◇

Jesus, You were fully man even as You were fully God. I can turn to You even when no one else is around, even when no one understands. You experienced great pain. You hung on the cross and gave Your very life for me. You died a painful death.

◇◇◇

God, I thank You for medical professionals and others who assist me, and I pray that You will guide them as they treat my pain. At times the illness and discomfort get the best of me. I need You to be in control and to help me, Father.

◇◇◇

God, this pain has taken control of my life. I feel weak and helpless. Discouragement, frustration, and resentment threaten to drown me. Lord, please show me the way forward. Allow me to find ways to control this pain. Teach me how to live with it. Transform it into something that leads me closer to You.

Christ Jesus, You suffered greatly. I am not alone in
this suffering. Help me never to forget that.

◇◇◇

One day there will be no more tears. One day I will run and
dance and enjoy a new, flawless body. I will spend eternity in
heaven with You. For now, remind me that You are near.
Touch my weary brow. Restore my hope, I pray.

◇◇◇

God, thank You that You are loving and slow to anger. Even
when I grow angry with You for not healing me, You remain
faithful to me until the anger takes its course and is replaced
with a renewed hope and a rejuvenated faith. I'm sorry
for being angry. I know that You are a good
Father and that I am deeply loved by You.

◇◇◇

Father, I am tired of hurting all the time. I admit that I wonder
why You haven't answered the prayers sent up for my healing.

◇◇◇

Forgive me for my pride, for thinking I have to face this alone.
Help me let people in, trusting that You can use my pain as
part of what You're doing in their lives, and use
them to lessen my loneliness and pain.

◇◇◇

Christ, I choose to treat this pain as a way I can partake in Your
sufferings. I believe that when Your glory is revealed to me,
I will also share in Your gladness and joy (1 Peter 4:13).

When I'm discouraged, Lord, remind me that today's suffering is nothing compared to the new work You are performing within me, a shining glory that will one day be revealed (Romans 8:18).

◇◇◇

Some days, God, I have to confess that I feel angry with You. Why are You doing this to me? Why won't You take my pain away? Thank You, dear Lord, that You are big enough to handle my anger.

◇◇◇

God, I feel so alone in my pain. The emotions it causes are harder to deal with than the physical aspect (which is no picnic either). Strengthen me in my spirit, then, so I can better deal with the signals my body is sending. Build hope in my heart that I can be more like Jesus because of this. Teach me that contentment in this life is always elusive, that I need to look beyond my circumstances to see something eternal: the love Jesus Christ demonstrated for You and for others. Thank You for the fellowship I have with You in my suffering (Philippians 3:10).

◇◇◇

Jesus, I don't know how to obey the apostle Paul when he tells us to rejoice in our sufferings. I will wait on You, though, believing that somehow this suffering will produce endurance. . .and endurance will produce strength of character. . .and that hope will grow out of that, a hope that will never be disappointed. Thank You for pouring Your love into my heart through the Holy Spirit (Romans 5:3–5).

◇◇◇

God, I cast this burden of deep pain on You. I ask You to sustain me (Psalm 55:22). I need You, Father, like never before.

CHURCH DISCORD

There are six things the LORD hates—no, seven things he detests: haughty eyes, a lying tongue, hands that kill the innocent, a heart that plots evil, feet that race to do wrong, a false witness who pours out lies, a person who sows discord in a family.

PROVERBS 6:16–19 NLT

We often have high expectations for our church community. After all, church is the place where we expect to learn about God, the place where we assume God's love will be most evident to us. So when arguments and division disrupt our church, we may feel not only disappointed but also disillusioned. A church is a human organization, however, and all humans, at one time or another, fall short of what God wants for them.

What scripture makes clear though is that God has no patience with church arguments that spill over into gossip and backstabbing, factions and plots, outright lies and ever-accelerating hostility. It's all too easy to get sucked in—to take sides, to listen to the gossip, and even to contribute to the exaggeration and complaints that thrive in a divided church.

Conflicts are bound to happen in any family, including church families. But God's Spirit always seeks to heal and restore unity. As Christ's followers, we are called to be open to the Spirit's leading us. . .to build peace rather than strife!

Father, I am so frustrated with what I see at church.
We've forgotten that You made us to be in relationship with
You and with each other. Even though relationship with
other people has its challenges, it also has its rewards.
Forgive us for losing sight of Your desire for us to live life
with one another, to be different than the world—
and forgive me if I've contributed to it in any way.

◇◇◇

Jesus, I want to be a godly person. When I'm working with
others, it's so hard for me to avoid arguments, even in a
church setting. Help me to have a loving attitude.

◇◇◇

God, often I don't realize I'm part of the problem when I'm
just listening to gossip. I get interested in what's being said and
it draws me in slowly. Before I know it, I'm commenting and
making assumptions. Sometimes I even pass on the information
whether or not I know it's accurate. Please, Father,
help me to call this what it is. Gossip.

◇◇◇

Dear Lord, make me a peacemaker. Give me the words
to say that will build bridges between the groups
and individuals who are in conflict.

◇◇◇

Jesus, I don't want to be part of the problem within my
church. And yet it's all too easy to be sucked in to the gossip
and complaints. I find myself interested, wanting to know
more. . .and then before long, I realize I'm fanning the fires
of disagreement. I'm part of the very problem I hate so much.
Help me to resist. May I never sow discord within my church.

Heavenly Father, help me to build others
up rather than tear them down.

◇◇◇

Lord, it's hard for me to give in when I have a strong opinion
of how something should be done. It may be in the children's
ministry or even something as simple as how dishes should be set
out at a church dinner. Remind me that these are trivial matters
and that far more important is my ability to get along
with the others in my church fellowship.

◇◇◇

God, if we argue within our church family, how are we any
different than the world? The world sends us messages every
single day that revolve around self. Do it if it feels right.
Have it your way. Just do it. Your ways are not the ways of
the world; therefore, our church should stand out
as a holy place that revolves around love.

◇◇◇

Help me to avoid arguments and quarreling, but also
help me to remind others that negative words only cause harm
and divide the church. You want unity in the essentials,
liberty in nonessentials, and charity in all things.

◇◇◇

Heavenly Father, season my speech with Your gracious salt.
Give me wisdom to know how to answer each person.
Let me seek to use every conversation as a
step toward peace (Colossians 4:5).

I pray that my church will seek to humbly work together
in love and consideration that we might be pleasing to
You. Help us to be a peaceful church so that the lost
might enter our doors and find Jesus here.

◇◇◇

I want to sow seeds of kindness, joy, and spiritual truths.
I want to be part of something bigger than myself. I want to
use my gifts to further the kingdom, Jesus. Help me
never to sow seeds of discord in my church.

◇◇◇

How can we serve You, Jesus, when we are not serving one
another? Give the people of my church servants' hearts.
Set before us a picture of You washing Your disciples' feet.
May we serve one another. May we serve tirelessly in
your church as Martha, and yet never be too
distracted to sit at Your feet like Mary.

◇◇◇

It's easy, Lord, to trivialize the arguments in our church.
But this discord is truly a work of darkness, for it diminishes the
effectiveness of Your Body. We are called to bear fruit for You—
and these arguments are nonproductive and barren. May Your
Spirit use me to shine light on this conflict, so we can begin to
see its true nature. Transform this situation, Lord, I pray,
and may it begin to bear the lasting fruit of Your Holy Spirit.

◇◇◇

Jesus, how can we claim to have fellowship with You if
we're walking in darkness? We're not practicing the truth;
we're telling ourselves lies. Show us Your light, Lord, so that
we can walk in it. Restore our fellowship with one another.
Wash us clean of anger and division. (1 John 1:6–7)

Lord, give me the discernment to identify troublemakers and the courage to confront them—to "note those who cause divisions and offenses, contrary to the doctrine which you learned, and avoid them" (Romans 16:17 NKJV). When I can't avoid them, give me the words to remind them that You want unity in the church, and "to stop fighting over words. Such arguments are useless, and they can ruin those who hear them" (2 Timothy 2:14 NLT).

◇◇◇

God, our church has prided itself on separating itself from the world's immorality. We're not greedy, we tell ourselves smugly; we don't swindle people; we don't worship the world's false gods. And yet all the while that we've been so proud of ourselves, we've let these same sins into our midst. We've been greedy for our own way within our church. Give us eyes to see, Lord—and humble hearts that are willing to change.

◇◇◇

We come to You—the Living Stone that humans rejected but God chose—and we ask that we too be living stones, so that You can use us to build a spiritual house. We would be holy priests, offering up spiritual sacrifices acceptable to God. (1 Peter 2:1–5)

◇◇◇

Father, I find myself tempted to give into divisive behavior at church, but I will take the high and narrow road because that's Your path, Jesus, and I want to be more like You.

CRYING OUT TO GOD

In my distress I called upon the LORD, and cried unto my God: he heard my voice. . .and my cry came before him, even into his ears.
PSALM 18:6 KJV

Crying out to God is an act of desperation. In the Bible, whenever we read that someone cries out to God, it is also a fervent expression of faith and trust. Just as a baby cries, knowing that at the sound of its voice, the mother will respond, crying out to God expresses our confidence in His love, as well as His power to act on our behalf. It expresses our humility, surrender, and faith.

And God hears our cries. The Bible is filled with examples of times when God answered the cries of His people. Like a loving mother, He comes to us when we cry for Him. He will not leave us to cry alone.

Without You, Lord, I can do nothing (John 15:5). Help me!

◇◇◇

In my distress I called upon You, Lord, and I cried out to
You—and You heard my voice out of Your temple.
My cry reached Your ears (Psalm 18:6).

◇◇◇

"Jesus, Son of David, have mercy on me!" (Mark 10:47 NKJV).

◇◇◇

Fulfill the desire of my heart, dear God. Hear my cry
and save me (Psalm 145:19)!

◇◇◇

Lord, I need help. I ask for restoration of body and
mind, increased faith, and new strength. You are my
Lord, my Savior—and my healer, my friend.

◇◇◇

It is because of Your mercy, Lord, that I am not consumed,
because Your compassion never fails. Your love for me is new every
morning. Great is Your faithfulness (Lamentations 3:22–23).

◇◇◇

God, I am tired, sad, abandoned, beaten, and hopeless. I come to
You. All I can give You are broken pieces. Make me new again, I pray.

◇◇◇

Help! Sometimes that's the only word I can think of to pray.
You always hear my cry—even when all I can say is a single word.

◇◇◇

I'm lost! Please come and find me, Lord. I need You!
Bring me back into Your presence. Show me the way.

DEATH OF A CHILD

Blessed are those who mourn, for they will be comforted.
MATTHEW 5:4 NIV

When parents die, their children are called orphans; when a spouse dies, the remaining partner is a widow or a widower; but when a child dies, the English language has no word for the parents who are left behind. This is the loss for which even our language is unprepared. It goes against the natural order. It strikes at our very identity as parents, for our job was to give life, and then to nurture and protect that life—and now we seem to have failed.

This is a loss too terrible to be borne, too immense to be transformed by life's relentless movement forward. We may feel guilty even trying to find a way to heal and go on. We cannot believe that life will ever again hold joy or hope.

And yet Christ's promise in the Beatitudes belongs to us now. As strange and impossible as it may seem, His happiness will be ours, for He will give us courage and comfort even in the midst of sorrow. We do not know how to go forward, but we don't have to know. He knows.

Heavenly Father, through my child You taught me
how to love. Now, teach me how to grieve and to heal.
You give and You take away, but I will still praise Your name.

◇◇◇

Father, did You cry when Your Son died?
Do You understand what I'm feeling now?

◇◇◇

Father, thank You that the waves of grief are just that—waves.
Thank You for mercifully seeing to it that there are moments
of relief. They're few and far between right now, but they
do come. I thank You for those moments of relief.

◇◇◇

No one hurts like I hurt. I was this child's mother. I felt the
pains of labor when this life began, and I cry out in horror as
I have been forced to watch it end. Thank You that despite this
deep pain, I do know that in You there is no end to life.
I will see my beloved one again in heaven.
This is a promise I cling to today.

◇◇◇

I feel as though I've set out on a journey off the edge of the
world, Lord. All my hopes and dreams and plans are gone.
I don't care about any of them, now that my child is dead.
I don't understand. I don't know where to turn. Help me.

◇◇◇

I know they mean well, but their words sting. Others just don't
know how to deal with this. I don't either. Please help me to
be gracious and forgiving when their words are all wrong.
They mean well, Father. They know not what they
do when they say these things to me.

Nothing makes sense anymore, Father. Thank You that it is enough for me to be silent before You. I have no words, and I cannot pray. Not today. Thank You for assuring me that it's okay to just be still and to be held close today.

◇◇◇

I must eventually find a new normal. God, will You help me? This doesn't feel normal at all—trying to go on, trying to live when my child is not with me. I need Your help to make it through the day. I need You to help me find a new way to live.

◇◇◇

I know that those around me are grieving for my child as well, God. And yet my own grief is unique, for the bond I shared with my child was all my own. Thank You for understanding when no one else does.

◇◇◇

Jesus, I live in the hope of resurrection. You've promised that You are working all things together for good, and while I can't begin to imagine how my child's death fits into that, I know that when I see You, I will be reunited with my precious one.

◇◇◇

But I'm not done with grieving. I will never be done with grieving for my child. I cannot move on, because to do so would mean to leave my child behind. I will never again be the person I once was. I can't be. But Lord, I know You still have a purpose for me. Please reveal that purpose to me. Use this grief to transform me into a new instrument of Your love. May my life be a living memorial to my child. Even more, may it be what You want it to be. Give me strength to place my grief in Your hands.

Sometimes, God, it brings me just a bit of comfort to know that You lost Your Son too. You watched Him hang upon a cross and die a terrible death He did not deserve. You gave Him up willingly for us. I can trust You because Your comfort is not just sympathy but empathy. You too have buried a child.

◇◇◇

God, I know this grief is the price I pay for having loved with all my heart. I don't regret loving my child with the love only a mother can give. I would do it all again even if I knew it was going to end. I would love just the same. I would pour out myself just the same way. How I miss the privilege of being a mom to my child. Hold me, Father, as I mourn this deep, deep loss.

◇◇◇

Lord God, I'm so grateful for the time You gave me with my child. In the time we had, I was changed forever. My heart was made fuller, my eyes were opened wider, and my faith was made stronger. I'm overwhelmed with fond memories and gratitude, which I will carry for the rest of my life in a way that honors my dear one and You.

◇◇◇

God, I'm struggling to find words. I don't know what to pray, how to pray, or, honestly, even *why* to pray. I can't imagine why You let my child die. Right now, it's best if I let You pray. "But if we hope for what we do not see, we wait for it with patience. Likewise the Spirit helps us in our weakness. For we do not know what to pray for as we ought, but the Spirit himself intercedes for us with groanings too deep for words" (Romans 8:25–26 ESV).

Just when I think I'm finally getting a handle on life again,
Lord, I'm overwhelmed all over again with sorrow. One moment,
I'm coping. . .and the next, I'm sobbing. Sometimes I feel too
depressed to get up in the morning. Other days I feel filled
with rage at others, at life, at You. God, lead me one step at a
time. Moment by moment, I'm depending on You.

◇◇◇

Lord Jesus, thank You for memories. Show me how to delight
once more in my child's life. I am so grateful that You created
this special individual and that I had the privilege to be this
child's parent. Help me to trust this child to You now, knowing
that my child was never truly mine. This child was always Yours.

◇◇◇

Lord, this is not a simple situation, but then You are not a
simple God. Right now, all I have to offer You is my tears, none
of which seem to fill the emptiness in my heart. I trust that You
are grieving with me, that You are in fact "a man of sorrows,
acquainted with deepest grief" (Isaiah 53:3 NLT).

◇◇◇

Father, give me the strength I need to be there for my family.
I never thought I could hurt this much, but my spouse and other
kids still need me. They see me hurting, but they are grieving
too. They need me to be there through all the painful "firsts"
of our new normal—first birthday, first Christmas,
first beginning of the school year. I need to set the tone
for talking about my child with them and with others,
so I need Your Spirit and Your words more than ever.

DEATH OF A PARENT

I will not leave you as orphans; I will come to you.
JOHN 14:18 NIV

No matter how old we are when our parents die, we suddenly find ourselves feeling like scared little children. We've never known a world without our parents in it. Even if we weren't close to them, they were still the most primary foundation of our lives. We are linked to them by invisible bonds that live within our very cells, and their deaths can shake us to the very core.

We may sometimes feel as though those around us don't truly understand our loss. Particularly if our parents were elderly when they died, others may expect us to accept their deaths easily. "After all," we'll hear, "they had a good long life." But clichés like that are small comfort to that frightened child inside our hearts.

But God understands. He is ready to meet us in a new way in the midst of this grief. He will not leave us as orphans.

Father, I am so grateful for the time I had with my parents, for all the memories, and for everything they taught me, especially about You. Even though I miss them terribly, the thought of them being with You, healed and whole, blesses me tremendously. Thank You for the hope of the resurrection, of the reunion to come, and of peace in the face of grief.

◇◇◇

Even as I grieve, Lord, and miss my father terribly, I'm thankful for him. I want to honor him, and I want his legacy of godliness to continue in me and in my children.

◇◇◇

Father, I'm thankful for the memories, but they bring me little comfort today. Instead, they hurt. I miss my parent. I miss all the happy times. I pray that one day I'll be able to enjoy the memories again without the pain. Bring me through grief to the other side, I pray.

◇◇◇

God, regardless of my parent's imperfection, this was the parent You gave me. In all our ups and downs, this was my parent still. Help me to honor the memory of my parent as I walk through this time of loss.

◇◇◇

Father, I'm shaken by this loss. It's one that goes all the way to my core, for my parents were with me from the beginning. I really don't want to find out what it's like to be without them, but I have no choice. Help me, Father. I feel so sad today.

Father, I thought I was so independent and mature.
But the death of my parent makes me see how
much I need You. Be with me now, I pray.

◇◇◇

Lord, I've been trying to push that scared child inside me to one side. After all, I've been a grown-up for a long time now! But today, I give that child to You. Help me to honor that child's fears—and maybe even listen to the perspectives that child has to offer on my life today. Comfort that child as I grieve for my parents.

◇◇◇

Dear God, I am who I am largely because of my parent, and now I am without this vital person in my life. Help me to remember all the lessons I learned just through doing life together with my parent for many years. Help me to honor my parent's memory by being a beautiful legacy as their child in this world.

◇◇◇

Jesus, there are words I wish I'd spoken and hugs I wish I'd given. There are visits I wish I'd made more effort to make happen. There are cards that were not mailed and phone calls I was too busy to place. Please take away my guilt and remind me today of all the things I did do right for my parent.

◇◇◇

I'm shaken, God. It's hard for me to think of myself as an orphan. I'm so used to being independent, even to being the one who helped out my parents. But it's hard to believe they're gone. If I'm honest, I feel a little like a kid again, scared of the dark because the people who taught me to face it are gone.
I know You are with me, though, and I'm glad.
I need You now more than ever.

Dear God, thank You for my parent's life. Thank You for all the ways You loved me through them, all the things You taught me, all the ways You've blessed me. I treasure the memories that I have. Let me continue to learn from my parent, even now that this beloved person is no longer with me in this life.

◇◇◇

I feel guilty, Lord. I could have been a better child. I could have done more for my parent. I could have better shown my parent my love. And now it's too late. Lord, I know I can't change the past. And so I give it to You. Help me to let it rest in Your hands.

◇◇◇

I guess I always knew my parents may die before I did. It's sort of expected. But knowing it would happen and experiencing it are very different things. I had no idea how painful this would be. Give me the strength to walk through this grief. Give me love and support, I pray, at just the right moments, whether from my spouse or friends or coworkers. You know exactly what I need in order to survive this.

◇◇◇

Nothing comes to me that You have not allowed, God. Even this deep loss of my parent was ordained by You. Your Word says You have ordained each day that we live. You number them. My parent lived the exact number of days that You established. That brings me comfort. It reminds me that You are in control and even now, when nothing seems right, You are holding things together and will continue to do so.

God, I don't know if my parent was a believer. I will trust that to
You. As Abraham said, "Should not the Judge of all the earth do
what is right?" (Genesis 18:25 NLT). The thought of the "right
thing," though, is painful. It puts a knot in my stomach and
a lump in my throat. Help me to see Your justice—to see
that You are holy, that You are good, and that You don't
do anything that won't someday make sense.

◇◇◇

Now that my parent is dead, Lord, I find myself remembering
so many different stages of my life. The parent who held me and
kissed me when I was very small. The parent who taught me how
to tie my shoes and ride a bicycle. The parent who taught me
how to drive—and who filled me with resentment when I
was a teenager. The parent I learned to respect in new ways as
an adult. And the parent I watched grow old. Loving Lord,
let me carry my parent with me always in my heart.
Thank You for giving me this precious parent.

◇◇◇

I wasn't prepared for how much this would hurt, Jesus.
Please walk with me through this grief. Let me allow
this grief to teach me what You would have me learn.

◇◇◇

I'm feeling guilty, Lord, thinking of missed opportunities.
I didn't do everything I could have for my parents. I didn't love
them the way I should have, didn't spend the time with them.
And now they're gone. I own that, but I can't bear the weight.
Forgive me, Father. Teach me how to live with what I can't
change, how to leave those regrets and hard feelings
with You. Show me how to make things right
with the people in my life now.

DEATH OF A PET

Weeping may last through the night,
but joy comes with the morning.
PSALM 30:5 NLT

Our pets are part of our families. When they die, it's only natural that we feel sorrow and grief, just as we do when a human we love dies. And yet this is a loss that not everyone will understand. After all, it was "just an animal." Some people feel it's inappropriate to express sorrow for the death of a pet.

But God created these animals of ours. God loves them more than we do (how could it be otherwise?). He understands our sorrow when they die. And He will comfort our hearts.

God, may my children learn wisdom as they sorrow. May they
not be afraid to love again, even though all love leads to loss.
May they open their hearts to Your creation and to You.

◇◇◇

Lord God, I feel a strange push-pull at the loss of my pet. I miss
him terribly, but it's hard to share that with people who see my
grief over the loss of an animal as silly or unimportant. But I
know what my pet meant to me. And I know that You are a giver
of good gifts. Thank You for the time I had with my pet, for all
the memories and companionship. And thank You for giving
me a chance to love another living being so selflessly.

◇◇◇

Dear Lord, I miss my pet. When I come home, the house
seems empty, as though there's a hole in it now.
Please comfort me, I pray.

◇◇◇

I know my pet was an animal, not a human being—but
nevertheless I learned about You from my pet. My pet showed
me unconditional love. My pet delighted in my presence.
I never bored my pet nor was my pet ever too busy to spend
time with me. You showed me Your love through
this little one. Thank You, Lord.

Father, my family is grieving the loss of our beloved pet.
As each of us mourns in our own way, I want to set the right
tone—a healthy recognition of what our companion
meant to us along with a healthy process of grieving.
Give me the right words to say to my family.

◇◇◇

Heavenly Father, thank You for the gift of my pet's life.
I am grateful that You brought this animal into my life.
I treasure the memories, and I am grateful that they are mine.

◇◇◇

Creator God, You were the One who made this animal
in the first place. So now I trust this creature back to You.
I place my pet in Your hands, trusting in Your love.

◇◇◇

You created my pet, God. You breathe life into every living
creature, and You know just how long we are to spend on this
earth. I know You loved this little animal even more than I did.

Dear God, I miss my pet. There's such an emptiness in the house. When I come home, I feel so alone. Please comfort me as I grieve.

◇◇◇

When my spouse was too busy with work, my pet was there. When the kids ran off with friends, I always had the company of this special pet. I was always enough for him. There was a special bond that I terribly miss now. I know You understand my sadness, God. Please help me move through this time of grief to the other side where I can smile again and perhaps even enjoy owning a new pet.

◇◇◇

Lord, as I mourn the loss of my pet, I think of the lessons about unconditional love You taught me during our time together. That wonderful animal greeted me with enthusiasm, sought comfort in my presence, and enriched my life through a whole slew of memorable moments. My pet had nothing to offer me in terms of financial gain, corporate advancement, or social status, but his presence gave me joy.

God, thank You for giving me my pet and allowing me to learn from this special little one. Thank You for the lessons I learned through being loved so completely by an animal. Thank You for the memories. I would do it all over again even though I have to experience this sadness and grief.

◇◇◇

Thank You, God, that I've been given a sensitivity to others who have lost pets. I've been in their shoes. I understand the devastating loss. Help me to be there for others when they are experiencing the pain of losing a beloved animal friend.

◇◇◇

As much as I grieve over our pet's death, Lord, I know it is even harder for my children. Show me how to help them in this sorrow. May we together open our hearts to the pain of loss, knowing that You will be present with us in the pain.

Help me to find a way to carry my pet's memory with me, Lord. May I find joy and comfort in remembering.

◇◇◇

God, I am devastated at the loss of my pet. I loved my pet without condition or reservation, and in this imperfect, broken world, I feel the loss of that as much as anything. I need Your comfort, Lord.

◇◇◇

I feel a little emptiness now that my pet is gone. I need to be needed the way she needed me. That may sound odd because I'm so busy, but I miss caring for our pet. Bring me comfort and fill in that gap with Your love today, I pray.

◇◇◇

God, may my children learn through this. May they realize that love often leads to loss but that it's always worth it. Teach all of us, Lord, to be open to loving another pet, I pray.

DEATH OF A SPOUSE

Be merciful to me, LORD, for I am in distress; my eyes grow weak with sorrow, my soul and body with grief.
PSALM 31:9 NIV

After facing life as a couple, it's so hard to be alone again. Not only do we miss the one we love, but we're faced with so many practical challenges. We have to deal with a new financial reality. We have to take over the household responsibilities that our spouse handled. We may have to continue to be a parent, but now without the support and input from our spouse. And all while we're forced to cope with these day-to-day concerns, our hearts are breaking inside us. We've lost the person with whom we were most intimate, our lover and our friend. Emotionally, spiritually, and physically, we are in pain.

There is no quick and easy way through this time. Grief has no shortcuts. But God has promised to be with us, always. Nothing can separate us from His love—and He will walk with us, day by day and moment by moment, as we travel on grief's journey.

I feel like I'm always wet with grief, Father. Sometimes the water just dampens my feet, and other times it covers me. The water is high today, Lord, and I'm too weak to tread it, much less swim. Hold me up and help me to keep breathing. "Heal me, Lord, and I will be healed; save me and I will be saved, for you are the one I praise" (Jeremiah 17:14 NIV).

◇◇◇

Lord, I pray for wise and kind helpers who will walk with me and guide me through these difficult days—but I also ask that You would send Your Spirit to give me strength for all that needs doing. May I rely on You to get me through.

◇◇◇

God, I never expected to be walking through this. It feels as if You've left me all alone. How could this be? It doesn't seem real. But I wake up day after day only to find that it is, in fact, very real. My husband is gone. I feel abandoned. Be my husband, I pray. I am so heartbroken. Be the lover of my soul. Fill in all the empty spaces with Your love, Jesus. I need Your help to make it. I cannot do this alone.

◇◇◇

God, they made meals, but I could not eat. They sat with me, but I had no words to speak. I don't know how the hours passed because I'm just so numb. But I thank You that they came, these loving servants who have poured milk for my children and run errands and made necessary arrangements. Thank You that they came. They were Your hands and feet today.

Jesus, You told me to love my enemies, but I am glad that death is the enemy I don't have to learn how to love. In the last day, when You return and humble all Your enemies, "the last enemy to be destroyed is death" (1 Corinthians 15:26 NLT). I rejoice now that the foe that took my spouse—even if it's just for a season—will be conquered. By Your resurrection, You have taken death's sting forever, and I look forward to the day in eternity when You hold one hand and my spouse holds the other.

◇◇◇

God, nothing seems right anymore. No one says the right thing. I don't expect them to. There is nothing right to say. Everything feels off, and I feel so very alone. I need him. I didn't always appreciate him or tell him I loved him, but I need him, Father. He has abandoned me in this world. Bring me comfort, I pray. The pain is so deep, so intense. You are my only hope.

◇◇◇

I was not a perfect spouse, Lord. I wish I'd made more effort in some areas and held less tightly to a few grudges. Help me to know that no one is perfect. Help me to find peace in the sweet memories and to recognize that I did my best to be a good partner.

◇◇◇

God, how am I supposed to handle social situations now? People act so uncomfortable around me. They act as though if they pretend my spouse isn't dead, I won't remember either. They tiptoe around me awkwardly. Help me to forgive them, Lord. I know I've probably acted the same way to others. Please send me someone who will let me cry, who will give me a hug, and who will sit and listen as I talk about the one I lost.

Lord, thank You for reminding me through friends and loved ones to take care of myself. Others need me. You need me. I cannot lose myself completely in this. I must rely on You to see me through just as You've seen me through other seasons of difficulty. This seems too big, but nothing is too big for my God.

◇◇◇

Thank You for the honor of being his wife. Thank You for a wedding day photo that captured the moment. Thank You for our children who have his expressions and his passion. May we live out his legacy in this world. Thank You for the time we had with this special man. Help us to trust Your timing even though it seems he left us far too soon.

◇◇◇

O God, I can't face the calendar anymore. Anniversaries, Valentine's Day, birthdays, Christmas. . .they all bring memories and fresh pain. I miss my spouse in new ways with the passing of the seasons. I can't help but think, Last year at this time, we were. . . And I resent the passage of time, because each day takes me further away from the days I shared with my spouse. Lord, I give my days to You. May I seek You in each one, even the ones that are most painful.

◇◇◇

God, I'm numb. Saying I miss my spouse is a little like saying I miss breathing normally. Everything is just off. I don't know what thought scares me more—feeling nothing or feeling everything. Like the psalmist said, my flesh and my heart are failing, but You, God, are my strength (Psalm 73:26). You will give me what I need to keep going and to feel again in time.

Remind me, heavenly Father, even in the midst of my grief to take care of myself. It's hard to care right now. Nothing seems to matter very much. But I know others need me—You need me—and I need me (as funny as that sounds). Help me to take time to eat healthy meals. Give me the gift of sleep and relaxation. Remind me to exercise, even if it's just going for a walk.

◇◇◇

Thank You, Lord, for my spouse's life. I am so glad You brought this person into my life. Without this partner in my life, I would not be who I am today. Please continue to bless me through the memories I treasure of our time together.

◇◇◇

Father, help me to honor my wife by grieving her properly. I know she wouldn't want me to shut down, but sometimes I just have to. Even though I know she's with You, happy and pain-free, I'm still here, missing my friend, my lover, my helper. Jesus said, "Blessed are those who mourn, for they will be comforted" (Matthew 5:4 NIV). I will miss her for the rest of my life, but I know You still have things for me to do in this life, and she would want me to do them. That's all fine and good, but now I just need You to comfort me.

DENIAL

*Ye have purified your souls in obeying
the truth through the Spirit.*
1 PETER 1:22 KJV

Refusing to acknowledge that something is wrong is a normal way to cope with anything that puts our sense of control at risk—including a serious illness that threatens ourselves or those we love. A short period of denial can be helpful because it gives us time to absorb this new reality at a pace that won't send us into a tailspin.

But we can't linger in denial. Instead, we have to move on and face the truth, no matter how painful and terrifying it may be. Remember, though, God's Spirit dwells even here, in this truth we so desperately wish we could avoid. As we allow ourselves to become obedient to it, He will purify our souls.

Clear my thoughts, Lord, so I can focus on You. You know I don't want to accept this—but I believe You can use even this to Your glory.

◇◇◇

On the night before Your death, Jesus, You prayed, "Let this cup pass from Me" (Matthew 26:39 NKJV). But in the end, You faced what lay before You. You accepted the will of Your Father. Give me strength, I pray, to do the same.

◇◇◇

May the Trinity surround me now—Father, Son, and Spirit. Encircle me, I pray. Let me rest in Your reality.

◇◇◇

I know that when I am weak, dear Christ, You are still strong. Please renew my strength so that I can face the facts. May Your Spirit sing songs of hope within my soul. Awaken my heart, I pray, so that I may accept the truth.

◇◇◇

I struggle to think clearly, God—so I depend on Your Spirit to illumine my mind. I am afraid to face the darkness I sense gathering—so I look to You for light. I don't want to accept this heavy load—so I will give the burden to You. I wonder if I am strong enough to take what lies ahead—so I will rest for now in Your love and peace.

◆ ◆ ◆ ◆ ◆ ◆ ◆

DEPRESSION

The LORD is close to the brokenhearted and saves those who are crushed in spirit.

PSALM 34:18 NIV

◆

Depression is more than just the daily sadnesses that come and go. It's a deep-seated feeling that grabs hold of us and doesn't let go, day after day. It can take a toll on our social lives, our professional lives, our spiritual lives, and our health. Psychologists tell us that depression is the most common of all psychiatric disorders. Almost all of us, at one time or another in our lives, will experience it.

As Christians we may feel we should be immune to depression. But depression is no sin! God has promised us He will be especially close to us when we go through these bleak times. He will be there at our side, waiting to lead us into His joy once more.

I'm feeling low today, Father. The louder thoughts I'm having tell me I'm alone, that there's no way out. Turn up the volume of Your voice, Father. I'm desperate to hear from You, whether it's in Your Word or through someone else. Give me the strength the psalmist had when he wrote, "Why am I discouraged? Why is my heart so sad? I will put my hope in God! I will praise him again—my Savior and my God!" (Psalm 42:5–6 NLT).

◇◇◇

I'm waiting patiently for You, Lord. I know You will lean down to me and hear my cry. You will draw me up out of the pit of destruction, this miry bog of depression where I'm stuck. You will set my feet on the rock, and You will make my steps steady. And then You will put a new song in my mouth, a song of praise to God. Many will see what You have done for me, and they too will put their trust in You. (Psalm 40:1–3)

◇◇◇

I've been here before, God. Depressed. I know that last time there came a brighter day. You lifted me out of the pit. You took away the veil and revealed joy again...slowly at first, and then one day I could hardly remember the depressed state I had walked in for so long. Bless me with recovery again. Heal my mind and heart, I pray.

◇◇◇

I cannot imagine singing. I can barely get my shower and see to the duties of the day. But I have faith in You, Lord. One day I'll be on the other side of depression and I'll sing a new song. I'll tell of how You healed me and lifted me up. I'll sing a new song and it will be one of great joy and deliverance (Psalm 40:1–3).

Lord, I am beginning to think I'm depressed. Someone concerned about me brought up the possibility, but I hadn't wanted to admit it up till now. I've been through hard times before, but I've never felt like this—like things are getting worse and won't ever get better. I'm caught in a loop of emotions—sadness, anger, frustration, even despair—and it feels like my prayers are bouncing off the ceiling. Hear me, Lord. I'm trying to believe that You are with me; help my unbelief (Mark 9:24). Give me the courage to seek help. Please put someone in my path who can help me get a grip on this.

◇◇◇

Heavenly Father, why is my soul so cast down? Why do I feel such turmoil? Help me to hope in You. I know I will again praise You, for You are my salvation and my God. (Psalm 42:11)

◇◇◇

This is not my home. This world is full of trouble, including depression. But You, Jesus, have overcome the world. One day I will experience an existence in heaven that does not include the pain of darkness or this sick feeling of hopelessness. That will be a place of great hope. For now, there are troubles. You will walk us through them. I will keep my eyes on You, and one day I will be fully and forever free of these bouts of depression.

◇◇◇

God, give me wisdom. I don't always know what's best, and everyone has a different opinion on such things as counseling and medication. I know that I need help and admitting it is the first step. Help me to have the presence of mind, even in my depression, to make the best decisions that will help me to get well.

I feel like a failure, God. A loser. A bad Christian. I feel like an awful employee because of my lack of focus. I feel like a pitiful spouse and parent because I'm so sad all the time. I feel beat down. Please remind me of my identity in Jesus Christ. I claim today that I am deeply loved and that I am not a failure. Bring healing to my mind today, Jesus, just as You healed the bodies of those who dared to reach out and touch Your robe.

◇◇◇

God, I know You are with me, but I confess, I've been thinking some about what it would be like to be with You. . .in heaven. I know that You wouldn't want me to take my own life, but I just want the pain to stop. I can't manage it anymore. I don't want to die, but living hurts so much. Step in, God, and save me! "For the grave cannot praise you, death cannot sing your praise; those who go down to the pit cannot hope for your faithfulness" (Isaiah 38:18 NIV).

◇◇◇

Blessed be You, God, the Father of my Lord Jesus Christ, for You are the Father of mercies and the God of all comfort. You comfort me in all my affliction, including this depression that has me in its grip. Use me one day to comfort those who are going through something similar. May I pass along the comfort You give to me now. (2 Corinthians 1:3–4)

Jesus, thank You for coming to earth and sharing our human experiences. I know that in You I can find peace. In this world, I will run into hard times—but when that happens, I will take heart, for I know You have overcome the world. (John 16:33)

◇◇◇

Dear God, I am in an emotional desert, a barren and howling wasteland. Shield me, Lord. Care for me. Guard me as the apple of Your eye. (Deuteronomy 32:10)

◇◇◇

Lord, You reached down from above. You took and drew me up out of the deep waters of depression. You delivered me from my strong enemy, from this depression that was too strong for me to overcome on my own. When calamity seemed to surround me, You held me steady. You brought me forth into a large place, a place of freedom and emotional health. You delivered me, because I delighted You. (2 Samuel 22:17–20)

◇◇◇

Give me strength and peace, Lord. A lot's been going on, and even though I'm seeking help to fight this depression, today is just a black dog kind of day. I trust that You have Your reasons for allowing me to suffer this way, that You can use my hardship to comfort someone else in a similar space, and that You will make me stronger—or at least more willing and able to rely wholeheartedly on You. God, You are my healer, my redeemer, my friend. I need You today.

DISABILITIES

Then Jesus said to his host, "When you give a luncheon or dinner, do not invite your friends, your brothers or sisters, your relatives, or your rich neighbors; if you do, they may invite you back and so you will be repaid. But when you give a banquet, invite the poor, the crippled, the lame, the blind."

LUKE 14:12–13 NIV

The Gospels make very clear that God cares about people with disabilities. The people who are overlooked and separated from the rest of society are the very people to whom Jesus paid most attention. The Gospels are full of stories of Jesus healing people who are blind, unable to walk, or broken in some other way. We never hear of Him looking down on these people as being less important or less deserving of His time. Instead, He treated each one with respect and compassion—and then He raised them up, so that they could take their place in society once more.

As Christ's followers, we too are called to reach out to those with disabilities. We cannot heal their physical issues—but we can treat them with dignity and respect. We can make sure they are not overlooked or ignored. And we can work to bring them back into society, allowing them to contribute to our communities.

Jesus, I read in the Gospels how You went around restoring people's vision, giving back the ability to walk, allowing the deaf to hear, and healing every disability You encountered. I know it's not likely I can literally heal physical disabilities in the people I meet—but I pray that nevertheless, Your healing power would work through me. Dear Father, may I see You in each person, no matter how broken they may appear to be on the outside. May I remember that when I serve those who are disabled, I am truly serving You.

◇◇◇

God, sometimes I think I fear that which I don't understand. I see people with certain disabilities and I'm not sure how to react. Please help me to be loving and kind, treating everyone with respect and as I want to be treated. You love all of us, regardless of our race, age, or if we have a disability or not. Each of us is made in Your image.

◇◇◇

Lord, I feel like I'm on a roller coaster with this disability. Some days my emotions are stable, and I feel good. Other days I feel far from "normal," and I just wish I could do all the daily tasks that others do so easily. Please steady my thoughts and feelings. Help me to trust You to meet my needs, even with this disability, day by day.

◇◇◇

Dealing with this disability takes all my strength, Lord. I'm exhausted. I don't have anything left to give to anyone else. Renew my heart, I pray.

Lord, as a disabled person in a world that values independence and accomplishment, remind me that my value is not based on what I can do but on what You can do through me. You said You would use the things the world considers weak to trip up the things it considers strong (1 Corinthians 1:26–29). Let Your strength and wisdom mark my life, so that my disadvantage becomes an advantage in bringing You glory and in advancing Your kingdom.

◇◇◇

You are the Great Physician, Father. Whether You choose to heal me in this life or wait until I'm in heaven with a brand-new body, I trust You. I know that You will use this area of my life to grow me closer to You. My faith is stronger because I must look to You every day. Draw me close, and remind me that You are my confidence.

◇◇◇

Dear heavenly Father, sometimes I feel like all I can do is deal with this disability. I feel like daily life is somewhat of an obstacle course for me. I watch others who don't have disabilities, and I find myself feeling envious. Please remind me that everyone I meet is fighting some sort of battle. We are all imperfect and weak creatures in need of a strong God to carry us. Thank You for being my Savior and friend.

◇◇◇

You told the apostle Paul, Lord, that Your grace was all he needed. Your power, You said, is made perfect in weakness (2 Corinthians 12:9). Remind me to never look down on any form of disability as being weakness. Instead, let me always be open to Your power working in surprising ways.

I know that people see me as different and some of them feel sorry for me. I sense it when they stare. Some look at me in a sad way as if they don't know what to say. I want to thank You for my differences, God, even though at times they are a real challenge. They make me more sensitive to those around me. I realize all of us have special needs. Some are on the outside and some hide within. Help me to look at others with a smile and kind eyes.

◇◇◇

Father, I want to help those with disabilities. Show me what I can do even if it seems like a small gesture. Guide me to an opportunity within my church or community. Perhaps I could babysit children with special needs while their parents attend Bible study. Maybe I could help out with Special Olympics. Direct my path, I pray.

◇◇◇

Ultimately, Lord, I know that all of us, sooner or later, will likely encounter some form of disability, especially as we grow older. Disability is part of the human condition. I cannot separate myself from it. Instead, dear God, I pray that You will use my disabilities for Your glory.

◇◇◇

Father, it's hard for me to find a place to belong. I know I'm Yours, a member of the body of Christ, but people often don't know how to approach me. I know I'm different, but I also know You don't make mistakes. You made me like this for Your good reasons, and I want to serve You. I want to love and be loved by Your people, to be missed when I'm not there, and to be supported when things go wrong—and to miss others and support them in turn. I want to be Your servant in my community.

Jesus, thank You for touching and embracing those the world considers outcasts when You came to earth. In the world's eyes, it's a total long shot that someone like me could ever become much of anything. But in Your eyes, I'm worth Your very life. I want to see people who think I'm nothing through Your eyes and with Your heart, and love them with the grace You showed me.

◇◇◇

God, You have seen fit to bring someone with a disability into my life. I don't want to shirk the responsibility I have to treat everyone I meet with respect and honor (Philippians 2:3–4), but I admit I don't really know where or how to start. Your Word tells me "to do justly, to love mercy, and to walk humbly" with You (Micah 6:8 NKJV). I want to go beyond just including people with disabilities at church, but to also do what I can to make sure they know they belong and that we are willing to learn from their experiences and wisdom. Help me to listen well, to learn more, and to fight the distinction of "them and us." We are Your children, all of us valued parts of the body of Christ.

◇◇◇

Father, all of us deal with a disability at some point or another. Whether it's temporary or permanent, You're aware of it and Your purposes are in it. Such a time has come upon me. I'm having to take stock of how I saw myself before—all the things I thought made me important that I don't have or can't do now. Like Paul, I ask You for deliverance, relief, and healing— but like Paul, I want to embrace the truth that Your grace is sufficient for me (2 Corinthians 12:9).

DISAPPOINTMENT

Though the fig tree does not bud and there are no grapes on the vines, though the olive crop fails and the fields produce no food, though there are no sheep in the pen and no cattle in the stalls, yet I will rejoice in the LORD. I will be joyful in God my Savior.

HABAKKUK 3:17–18 NIV

Disappointment comes in all shapes and sizes. Maybe life itself has disappointed us. We had hoped to reach a particular milestone by this point in our life—and it hasn't materialized as we'd imagined. In fact, our goal is as far away as ever. We may have had to face that we will never attain it at all. Maybe someone we counted on has let us down, and we're disappointed that this individual is not the person we had thought. Or maybe it's our own selves that have disappointed us. Our own failures and weaknesses have forced us to realize that we're not the people we dreamed of being.

But one thing is certain: no matter what else disappoints us, God never will! When everything else lets us down—when the fig tree doesn't bud, the vines have no grapes, our crops fail, and everything in our lives is empty—we can still rejoice in God our Savior.

God, I'm bringing the weight of my disappointment to You. I did the best I could do—I prayed, read the Bible, sought godly counsel—and it wasn't enough to bring the result I wanted. I have all sorts of questions, but the one I need to be asking is, "What now, Lord?" Bring me something or someone to point out the next step, whatever it may be. I trust You.

◇◇◇

Father, I'm not where I thought I would be in life. I imagined things differently. I knew a prince would not ride in on his white horse, but I never expected my reality to be quite this mundane. There are dishes to be done and a house to keep clean. The laundry piles up around me. I pray that I'll work at everything I do today as if I'm working for You. Give me contentedness in the midst of disappointment.

◇◇◇

Lord, You know that things haven't turned out as I wanted. You saw the dream as it grew within my heart. You watched me get my hopes up. You were there as I held my breath, hoping for the answer I wanted so desperately. I wonder why You let it all slip through my fingers. Remind me that Your ways are higher than my own (Isaiah 55:8–9) and that You always have my best interest in mind.

◇◇◇

Lord, You know how disappointed I feel right now. Remind me, Lord, that I am Your child, and You have a lesson You want me to learn from all this. Help me not to lose heart. I know that even this disappointment comes to me through Your loving hand, because I am Your child. Just as my human parents had to say no to me sometimes, so that I could learn, You too are doing what is best for me.

Lord, help me to understand that my disappointment is not because You've let me down but because my expectations weren't met. I don't want to get on a roller coaster of resentment and cynicism, blame-shifting and grudge-holding my way to a bitter end. So, I'm giving You my sadness and disappointment because I don't want it to get the better of me. I don't want to stop giving my best or stop expecting the best from You or others. I trust that You are working all things together for good, taking into account all the details and issues and personalities that I could never be aware of or fully anticipate. I will expect You to be true to Yourself—and that's more than enough for me.

◇◇◇

Jesus, this test feels more like a dead end than just a bump in the road. I'm so disappointed. Yet I know that this trial will strengthen my faith and instill perseverance in me, helping me toward completeness (James 1:2–4). Please use even the disappointments in my life to make me more like You.

◇◇◇

Like Mary and Martha who waited for You to come and heal Lazarus, my jaw drops when You don't show up to rescue me or provide what I desire. Remind me that You are never early or late but always right on time. What feels like a disappointment is only a detour that will take me to something greater.

◇◇◇

Father, when You close a door in my life, You always open another one. Right now I'm so fixated on this one piece of the puzzle, but You see the completed picture. You know what is best. Help me to seek Your will.

God, I'm not the only one to be disappointed. When I look at the Bible, I see person after person who hoped for something—and then was disappointed. Abraham, Moses, David, the prophets—they all learned that disappointment is only temporary. What looks like a loss from my perspective now will one day be revealed as only the next step toward the amazing thing You were doing all along.

◇◇◇

Some trust in chariots—or, in present-day life, social media "likes" or promotions at work! I choose to trust in the Lord my God. When I feel let down and discouraged, remind me that You are my strength and my fortress. I am more than a conqueror through Christ.

◇◇◇

God, I like the song that says, "You are more than enough for me." I want that to be true in my life. When my spouse lets me down, when my children frustrate me, when my job is a disaster, You are more than enough. Please teach me to hold loosely to the things of this world that I might put my hope in You alone.

◇◇◇

Father, I am struggling to let go of my disappointment. All I can think of is the opportunity missed, the circumstances that resulted, and the people who let me down. And now I'm stuck in the *why* of it all. That's not where You want me to be, but I don't know how to get unstuck.

Jesus, help me to see the joy hidden inside this disappointment. I know that this testing of my faith will help me to develop the ability to persevere—and that ability in turn will allow me to grow up in You and become complete, not lacking anything. (James 1:2–4)

◇◇◇

Dear Jesus, whenever I cling to circumstances or people as my only happiness, I'm bound to be disappointed in the end. Help me to trust in You instead.

◇◇◇

Lord, I'm realizing that when I reach the point where I have nothing left but You, I can finally realize that You alone are enough. All my questions won't be answered in this life. My circumstances may not be improved. I'll have to let go of some of the things I've set my heart on. But none of that matters. You are the strength of my heart and my portion forever.

◇◇◇

Only You can meet all my needs, God. I'm caught between my expectations and my circumstances, and I'm not happy with either. I didn't think this is where I would be at this point in my life and I'm frustrated. I give my frustration to You, though. I want to "give thanks in all circumstances; for this is God's will for you in Christ Jesus" (1 Thessalonians 5:18 NIV). Thank You that I am Yours, that You make good things come out of bad things, that You have good plans for my future, and that You care about me right now.

DISCONTENTMENT

*I know what it is to be in need, and I know what it is to have plenty.
I have learned the secret of being content in any and every situation,
whether well fed or hungry, whether living in plenty or in want.*

PHILIPPIANS 4:12 NIV

Even the apostle Paul had to *learn* the secret to being content. It was not natural or innate; rather, it was *learned*. As we face circumstances that are less than desirable and find God there in the midst of our disappointment, we are strengthened in our faith. Can you look back to another time in your life, whether long ago or fairly recent, when God came through for you? He is in the business of making a way where there seems to be nothing but a dead end. That's how our God works.

So during this season of lacking or despair, look up. In this hopeless hole, claim hope in Christ your Redeemer. It may seem that you've been given the short straw or that life is nothing but a cruel joke. You may be nowhere near where you want to be today. But trust the heart of God. He is working out His plan in your life.

You were the King of the universe, and yet You were content to be laid in a manger as a baby. You were content to live an adult life in which You never really had a place to call home. You were content with the role God gave You. You asked Him to take the cup from You in the garden that night, and yet You were content to carry Your cross to Calvary for me if it was God's will. . .and it was.

◇◇◇

God, I know that contentment begins with an attitude change. I haven't been able to make it. I see glimpses of it at times, but my overall outlook is bleak, not sunny. I need to find a place of contentment. Show me the way. It seems so overwhelming, so out of reach. Show me just a small step that I can take today to become more content.

◇◇◇

Circumstances dictate my level of contentment. It shouldn't be that way but honestly, it is. When good things happen, I'm a happy Christian, praising You in church and singing and praying throughout the week. When hard times come, I blame You. I ask where You are. I turn away. Funny how when I come back around, You are always there. You haven't moved. I'm the fickle one. Create in me a more content spirit that I might be faithful to You regardless of my situation or my station in life.

God, when I see someone who is old or sick or in some way
disabled, I often find in their eyes a sense of contentment.
I see it in the way they smile or offer a word of encouragement to
someone else—even though they themselves are not doing all that
great. Help me to find that kind of contentment. I don't think
my countenance reflects peace. I want it too, Father.

◇◇◇

Help me, God, to just hold on and "fake it till I make it."
As I express gratitude to You for all of Your blessings, help my
discontentment melt into appreciation for Your provision.
If I have to force myself to thank You for three things each day,
I will, Father. In time, I believe You can change my heart.

◇◇◇

Thank You, God, that You promise in Your Word that You
will never withhold a good and perfect gift from those who walk
with You (Psalm 84:11). My emotions are getting the best of me
lately. I begin to believe, at times, that You don't want me to be
happy. You seem to be keeping me from my dreams! I know that
I can trust Your heart, though, and that this is just a lie Satan
wants me to believe. Help me to trust that You are in control
and that although You have closed these doors, You surely
will open the right ones that You are preparing for me.

DISHONESTY

*"I am the way, the truth, and the life.
No one can come to the Father except through me."*
JOHN 14:6 NLT

As Christ's followers, we are to walk in the truth (3 John 3), love the truth, and believe the truth (2 Thessalonians 2:10, 12). We are to speak the truth in love (Ephesians 4:15). Christ came to us full of grace and truth (John 1:14), but He went still further than that: He told us that He *is* the truth personified, the truth incarnate. We are to love the truth because it is Jesus. We are to stay close to it and follow after it, because that is the way we follow our Lord. If we are Christ's representatives, then those around us should know we always speak the truth.

Lord God, I confess my dishonesty. I have never thought of
myself as deceitful, but I see now that my dishonesty is a sin—
first and foremost, against You. I've misrepresented You. You're
a God of order, not chaos; light, not darkness; and truth, not
lies. All the dishonest ways I've tried to build myself up or satisfy
my desires have built walls between me and You, and between
me and others. The real me isn't as attractive as the image I've
created, but that image was an idol to my ego. I forsake it and
choose You. Nothing is hidden from You, and yet You still love
me. I want to live honestly before You. Even if it's a broken,
ugly version of me, at least it will be an honest one—
and that means a forgiven, redeemed me constantly
in need of Your grace and love.

◇◇◇

Loving Lord, I hate to admit this, but being honest isn't always
easy for me. Little lies slip out of my mouth so glibly. I don't
even think about them ahead of time. I tell myself they don't
matter. After all, I'm not lying about big things. I'm only lying
about trivial things, to make my life easier, to smooth over
awkwardness, to let me have my way without upsetting anyone.
Lord Jesus, remind me that You are truth. Teach me that
lying hurts Your Spirit. Help me to love the truth.

◇◇◇

Father, sometimes I not only lie to others with my words;
I also lie to myself in my thoughts. I criticize myself unjustly.
Or I go to the other extreme and excuse myself too easily.
I hide unpleasant truths away where I don't have to look
at them. Reveal the truth within me, God. Give me
the courage to be honest even with myself.

Father, forgive me for my lies. I've built an image of myself that reflects the incomplete image I've formed of You—someone who winks at little white lies, who sees half-truths as a necessary evil in a broken world. I thought I was getting ahead, but I've forgotten Your holiness—and that You call me to be like You. And You've never lied and never will. I want to fill my heart with Your truth instead: "Brothers, whatever is true, whatever is honorable, whatever is just, whatever is pure, whatever is lovely, whatever is commendable, if there is any excellence, if there is anything worthy of praise, think about these things" (Philippians 4:8 ESV).

◇◇◇

Lord, help me not to lie to anyone. Instead, give me the strength to shed my old self with its deceitful habits and instead put on the new self You have called me to put on. Renew in me the image of my Creator, so that I may become the true self You always wanted me to be. (Colossians 3:9–10)

◇◇◇

God, I've been affected by someone else's dishonesty. My reputation has suffered, and the thought of it makes me angry. I'm not saying I'm perfect, but I feel blindsided and I want to defend myself. My mind is a maze of arguments and frustrations, and I don't trust myself to represent You well right now. Will You defend me instead? Will You remember all the times and ways I've tried to stay true to You and Your Word, forgive me for the times I've failed, and uphold me for Your name's sake? I will wait on You.

Holy Spirit, lead me into the truth. Help me to act in truth and abide in truth (John 3:21; 8:44). May the belt of truth hold together my spiritual armor (Ephesians 6:14), protecting me always.

◇◇◇

God, I know You never lie, for You are the God of truth. I can trust You to never be dishonest with me. You always keep Your promises. But Jesus called Satan a "liar and the father of liars" (John 8:44 ESV). Remind me always that when I speak the truth, I am speaking Your Son's language—but when I am dishonest, when I mislead others in any way, I am speaking the language of my enemy.

◇◇◇

Lord, help me to own my mistakes and to think about what it's like to be on the other side of me. I've tried to cover my mistakes by shifting the blame or misrepresenting what others have said or done. I haven't fooled anyone, but I have broken trust. Forgive me for drifting from Your Word and ways. I want to be honest in my dealings, but it's a day-to-day process of making lots of small decisions—managing my time and expectations, circling back on hard issues—and trusting that You will bring good things when I make a habit of loving others by seeking their best welfare consistently, which You have called me to do.

◇◇◇

Remind me, Lord, that if I'm dishonest even in little ways, I am also dishonest in big ways. Help me to be faithful with the smallest things, so that people can count on me to be faithful with life's greatest things. (Luke 16:10)

DISTRUST

I will trust and not be afraid.
Isaiah 12:2 niv

Trust is essential to our psychological well-being. We first learned to trust as babies cared for by loving parents. That most basic level of trust was the foundation on which all our human relationships were built. It is also what makes us able to trust God.

But sometimes parents fail to teach their children how to trust. If our parents hurt us, we may not be able to trust others, including God. Or maybe a close friend or a spouse damaged our trust later in life. When someone who is important to us lets us down, we learn to distrust others. We find it hard to trust even God. We are constantly on guard, trying to protect ourselves against hurt.

God wants to heal our distrust. He knows we can never be whole until we can trust Him. We will never have intimacy—even with God—until we can learn to trust once more.

Lord, I acknowledge that I have the universal human tendency to trust myself rather than You, to rely on my own abilities and good intentions instead of Your sovereign goodness and care. You have called me to reflect Your love and Your desire for forgiveness and restoration, so help me to make things right with the people I've hurt.

◇◇◇

God, I trusted once, but I was let down and betrayed. I don't know that I can open my heart to anyone else. I have tried, but I keep putting up the walls again and again. Please help me to trust You so that I can learn to trust others.

◇◇◇

I say that I trust You, God, but deep down I hold on to the reins. I won't quite surrender all the control over my life. Help me learn to trust so that I can depend on others and on You, Lord. It's a lonely and difficult life without trust.

◇◇◇

God, my trust has been shattered. My distrust is a wound that lurks in the very basement of my heart. On the outside, I look like I'm okay. I can laugh and have a good time. I can even love. But I can't trust. Lord, clean out the basement of my heart. Help me to trust.

◇◇◇

I want to trust You, God. But I can't. I want to give You control over my life. But no matter how many times I say the words, I can't follow through on them. I feel stuck. I'm helpless to change. Lord, I know You can do the impossible. Work a miracle in my heart, I pray.

I know that there's an abundant life waiting for me. I get glimpses of it at times. I start to make commitments and decisions but then, like a mouse, I run back into my hole! How can I know for sure that things will turn out well? How can I trust that these people won't change their minds or give up on me? I'm tired of living like this. Please help me learn to trust.

◇◇◇

God, I should apologize to You because I don't trust You. You are the Maker of the universe. I believe that. I know that even though I only see in part, I am fully known by You. How is it that I can't seem to trust that You know the plans You have for me? Help me to relax and believe that You have a bright future in store, plans to bring me hope, not harm (Jeremiah 29:11).

◇◇◇

God, someone close to me has broken trust with me. It's painful to realize that this person isn't who I thought he was. I forgive him, but I ask for Your wisdom in dealing with him in the future. I also need to ask Your forgiveness, for I trusted this person's promises because they sounded good, and I didn't trust You enough to ask what You thought about them.

◇◇◇

I keep saying that I love You, Lord. But I realize now that love and trust go together. I can't truly love You until I trust You. And without trust, I will never truly experience Your love for me.

◇◇◇

God, You are the One who began a good work in me (Philippians 1:6)—and I know You will not walk away from me now. You will help me to grow in Your grace. . . until I learn to trust You absolutely.

Lord, I do trust You. But help me to trust You more.

◇◇◇

When I read the Bible, I see, dear God, that I'm not the only one who had this problem. Trust was just as hard for many of the great Bible heroes. Jonah, for example, ended up inside a big fish because he wouldn't trust Your commands. Father, thank You that You never abandon me, even when I fail to trust You. Even when I find myself inside life's "big fish," You are there with me. And just as You did with Jonah, You give me another chance.

◇◇◇

Father, I want to trust You with all of my heart. I want to learn to lean not on what I understand, but in all of my ways to acknowledge You and to submit to Your will. I know that when I trust You, You will make my paths straight before me. You will lead me and never let me go (Proverbs 3:5–6).

◇◇◇

There are those who can and should be trusted in my circles, Father. There are also some who cannot and should not be trusted. Grant me discernment in this area that I might know the difference. I need to know when to trust and when to guard my heart, but it's not always easy to see the wolves in sheep's clothing. Show me those people in whom I should trust, I pray, and help me to stay far away from those who wish to hurt me (Psalm 5:9).

Father, I am struggling to trust my wife. There have been past hurts, and I feel myself withdrawing from her. I feel like I have to be careful around her, that I can't rely on her to do what she says she will do. I often feel myself being critical of her, which is usually a sign that I need to check my own heart. Show me if I am being untrustworthy in any way—if I am not making her feel safe or cared for. Successful marriages are built on trust. Your Word says of a godly wife that the "heart of her husband trusts in her, and he will have no lack of gain" (Proverbs 31:11 ESV). We need honesty between us, even if it's painful at first, and accountability so we can move forward together.

◇◇◇

Lord, I am dealing with the fallout of broken trust. What someone has done constantly swirls around in my mind, and I'm struggling to control my hurt and anger. Your Word reminds me to trust in You with all of my heart and not to lean on my own limited understanding, but I need You to get me back on course (Proverbs 3:5–6). I need to let go and forgive this person. I don't want to become an untrusting person, but I need Your discernment so I can know whether to give the benefit of the doubt. Even if this person never regains my trust, I need to show the mercy and grace You've so often shown me.

◇◇◇

God, as I think about the difficult situation I'm in, and the disappointment and frustration I feel, I realize that this isn't Your fault but mine. As much as it hurts to say so, I haven't trusted You, even though You have saved me from sin and provided for me so many times and in so many ways. I tried to do this in my own strength and came up short. Forgive me.

DIVORCE/SEPARATION

There is no God like you in the skies above or on the earth below, who unswervingly keeps covenant with his servants and unfailingly loves them.

2 CHRONICLES 6:14 MSG

When a marriage fails, it hurts. Even if the relationship itself was damaged and unhealthy, the final breakup is painful. It forces us to face the loss of our dreams and hopes. We are full of disappointment and sorrow. And on top of that, we face new stress and responsibilities. Our routines and responsibilities have been disrupted and rearranged. Our relationships with others—children, extended family, friends, church members—may have been shaken as well. We may feel embarrassment and resentment alongside our sorrow and hurt. The future we had hoped for is gone, and we don't know what to hope for in its place.

All we can do is turn to God. In the midst of what seems like one of the biggest failures of our lives, He is there. He has not abandoned us. He still has plans for our lives. And His love for us will never fail.

Dear Jesus, I feel so many things all at the same time.
I'm furious and sad, exhausted and frustrated, confused and
relieved. Some days I don't feel anything at all, only numbness.
Thank You that whatever I'm feeling, You're always there with
me. You understand me even when I don't understand myself.

◇◇◇

My heavenly Father, thank You for Your patience with me
during this time. I just don't seem to be able to live up to my
usual standards right now. I can't get as much done. I seem
to have less energy. I don't feel like I'm much use to You
or Your kingdom. Lord, one day make me useful again.
In the meantime, I'll let myself drop into
Your hands. Please don't let me fall!

◇◇◇

Lord, divorce is not the unpardonable sin, but it's not what You
want for me either. I admit that there are times when divorce
seems like the only way to deal with my relationship with my
spouse. I know the current state of my marriage didn't develop
overnight, and I know it won't be resolved right away either.
Regardless of the cause, and regardless of whether there is
biblical support for ending my marriage, I commit
myself to seeking Your will for my marriage.

◇◇◇

God, it all just happened. It seemed to spiral out of control,
and then there were papers making it legal. . .and he was gone.
The end had come, and I hardly even had time to say goodbye.
Sometimes I wish he had died. I know that's an awful desire, but
I guess death is just "cleaner," more clear cut. This type of grief
is so confusing because my husband—my ex-husband—is still
living. Help me, Father. I am so confused and sad.

I'm grieving today, Lord—grieving for the loss of
companionship in my life, for the death of hopes,
for broken promises, and for plans that will never be fulfilled.
Give me courage to mourn my marriage. Give me strength
to place it in Your loving hands and leave it there.

◇◇◇

Everything in my world has been shaken, and it seems so odd
that the sun still comes up and everyone is moving on as if
nothing happened. Help me make it through each day,
Father. I feel so useless and out of control.

◇◇◇

God, help me not to be bitter about this divorce. I know that
bitterness can grow up and fester in my heart and that it has the
potential to ruin my life. I have seen others allow this to happen,
and I don't want to be like them—sitting around talking about
this for years to come. Give me strength to grieve well and
then to move forward well. Thank You, Father.

◇◇◇

God, I have not always walked in Your ways, and that is partly
why my marriage is falling apart. I have no peace and no joy at
the thought of getting separated or divorced, but I don't
know how to fix my marriage either.

◇◇◇

I know You still love me, God, but I don't know why. I feel
so used up and worthless now. I feel like all the promises and
dreams are just gone, over, done with. What happened?
I glanced at a wedding photo today. Where did those happy
smiles go? I had so hoped things would turn out differently.

Dear Jesus, I don't want to swallow my anger and hurt so that they fester inside me—but I also don't want to get stuck in them. I've gone over the past so many times, examining each mistake and hurt from every possible perspective. Help me to know when it's time to let it go—and move on into whatever You have for me next.

◇◇◇

Sometimes, Creator God, I feel as though my future died when my marriage did. I feel guilty even hoping to replace those old dreams with new ones. Help me to trust You. Help me to believe that You still have dreams for my life.

◇◇◇

I am desperate to avoid the emotional and spiritual tsunami that breaking up my family unit would cause. I need to remember that Your love lasts, that You keep Your commitments and expect me to keep mine, and that You can make a way where there seems no way. I want to break this cycle of divorce in my family history, but I can't do it without You.

◇◇◇

I feel like I need some help, Lord. I don't think I can move past this without assistance. If there's a certain friend or counselor I should turn to, please put that person in my path. Make it clear to me, I pray, if I should attend a support group. I want to heal, Father, and I need help.

◇◇◇

Holy Spirit, I want to show my spouse evidence of change, and I want to avoid separation or divorce. It'll take time, so help my mate to be as patient and gracious with me as You have been. Fill me, lead me, and give me the words to rebuild what's been damaged.

Help me to make wise choices when I consider whom to confide in about my divorce. I need to talk it through, and yet I don't want to discuss it with all of my friends. I can't reveal details to everyone. It isn't even right. My marriage was a private thing until this happened. Now I feel like everyone is wondering what happened and looking for answers. Help me to know when to speak and when to remain silent, Father. Give me discernment as I choose a friend whom I can trust to listen and remain confidential.

◇◇◇

Jesus, I need to take an unflinching look at how my behavior is damaging my marriage. You said that my spouse and I "are no longer two but one flesh. Therefore what God has joined together, let not man separate" (Matthew 19:6 NKJV). I have said things, looked at things, and done things that threaten to shatter a bond You meant to be permanent in this life. If You responded to me based on the way I've responded to my spouse, You would have revoked my salvation by now. I'm so grateful You never will, and I want for my marriage the forgiveness and reconciliation You offered me.

◇◇◇

Lord, I don't know how to move forward. I think I need help. Show me where to turn. Give me discernment to know if I need to talk to a wise friend—or if I need professional counseling to help me deal with this. Guide me to the right person who will shed Your light on my life.

DOUBT

Jesus immediately reached out and grabbed him.
"You have so little faith," Jesus said. "Why did you doubt me?"
MATTHEW 14:31 NLT

Peter was walking along on the surface of the water, his eyes fixed on Jesus, doing just fine. Suddenly, he realized what he was doing. He looked at the waves beneath his feet, and he knew that what he was doing was *impossible*. Instantly, his feet sank into the water. He knew he was going to drown.

But Jesus didn't let him. Our Lord grabbed His good friend and saved him. And He does the same for us, over and over, every time we're swamped with doubts and start to sink into life's depths. "Why do you doubt Me?" He asks us. "Have I *ever* let you sink?"

Lord, I am relieved that doubt and faith are not incompatible. But I'm having a hard time seeing You at work lately. I admit I've been disappointed in the way some things have worked out—things I prayed and searched Your Word about—but I sympathize with the dad in the Bible who prayed, "Lord, I believe; help my unbelief!" (Mark 9:24 NKJV).

◇◇◇

Jesus, I can't help but identify with Peter—and with Thomas too. I want proof that You will keep Your promises to me, that You are who You say You are, that You will help me to do the things that seem so impossible. Forgive me for doubting You.

◇◇◇

God, forgive me for doubting You. I don't want to be like Thomas who demanded tangible proof. He wanted to see the nail scars in Your hands before he would believe You. Your Word gives me all the promises I need. I know that. I want to believe. Help my unbelief (Mark 9:23–24).

◇◇◇

God, help me to build my house upon the Rock of Christ Jesus, not on shifting sands. I know that there is no stability in doubting. I want my hope to be steadfast and true. You are the Alpha and the Omega, the beginning and the end. Help me to trust You with these and with everything in between.

◇◇◇

I want to trust You, God. I want to give You all my fears. But no matter how many times I say the words, I can't follow through on them. I feel stuck. I'm helpless to change. Lord, I know You can do the impossible. Work a miracle in my heart, I pray.

I know, Jesus, that I am like a wave of the sea, driven and tossed
by the wind (James 1:6). Doubts are like a storm all around me.
But You say to me, "Why are you afraid, O you of little faith?"
(Matthew 8:26 ESV). You have the power to quiet the storm.

◇◇◇

God, You are the One who began a good work in me (Philippians
1:6)—and I know You will not walk away from me now.

◇◇◇

Lord, I do trust You. But help me to trust You more.

◇◇◇

God, You know I still have doubts. But despite my doubts,
I affirm that neither life nor death, neither angels nor any
spiritual power, neither height nor depth, nothing the future
holds—in fact, nothing whatsoever will ever be able to
separate me from Your love (Romans 8:38–39).

◇◇◇

I remain confident of this, Lord: I will see Your goodness
in the land of the living. I will wait for You and
take heart (Psalm 27:13–14).

◇◇◇

Lord, fill me with Your wisdom—the wisdom that is
wholehearted and straightforward, free from
wavering and doubts (James 3:17).

◇◇◇

When I begin to doubt You, Lord, bring to mind all the times
that You have answered my prayers. Sometimes this helps me to
remain calm and trust You even in the midst of circumstances
that seem impossible. You are the God of the impossible.

Father, I am beginning to understand that faith is not a matter of certainty but trust. I trust that You are good, sovereign, holy, loving, merciful, just, righteous, and gracious, and that if I search for You with all my heart, I'll find You (Jeremiah 29:13).

◇◇◇

Father, I want to have faith like the men and women I read about in the Bible. Often, I trust only in what I can see before me. I realize that You call me to faith in that which I have not yet seen (Hebrews 11:1). It's really not faith if I only believe in the tangible. I must trust in the intangible.

◇◇◇

God, I'm looking at the world around me and I see that it's a mess. I give You my fear and guilt and frustration—and my doubt that I can make any kind of impact for You. I'm not sure what else to do, except ask You to walk with me. Walk with me, Lord.

◇◇◇

God, I'm praying—not because I'm convinced it makes the difference; Your Word says it does—but because I'm more anxious that if I don't, my faith will fail. I talk to You and wait for an answer, but I can't tell whether You've responded. I'll accept any answer You give me; I just want to hear one.

Holy Spirit, I pray for the assurance of things hoped for,
the conviction of things not seen. By faith, I understand that
God created the universe by His Word, so that the visible world
was made out of things that cannot be seen. I know that by faith
Abel gave You the sacrifice You desired, while Cain, because of
his lack of faith, did not. Because of Abel's faith, I still hear his
voice speaking to me in the scripture. Because of Enoch's faith,
You took him to You, allowing him to skip over death.
If Noah had been full of doubts, he would never have built the
ark. Abraham and Sarah, Isaac and Jacob, they all had doubts—
and yet they all surrendered their doubts to You and
walked in faith, doing the impossible. Lord,
help me to do the same. (Hebrews 11:1–12)

◇◇◇

Dearest Christ, thank You for Your Body. Thank You that those
who are strong in Your Body help carry me when I am weak.
When I am full of doubt, I rely on their faith. Give me
strength one day to do the same for someone else.

◇◇◇

Heavenly Father, give me the ability to see beyond today
to the future that You have in store for me. Help me to
believe that You are not finished with me yet.

◇◇◇

Father, thank You for Your promises in scripture that I can
claim throughout my trials. You promise to never leave me or
forsake me. You assure me that nothing—absolutely nothing—
has the ability to separate me from Your love (Romans 8:38–39).

DRUG ABUSE

Do you not know that your bodies are temples of the Holy Spirit, who is in you, whom you have received from God? You are not your own; you were bought at a price. Therefore honor God with your bodies.

1 CORINTHIANS 6:19–20 NIV

Our bodies are the Holy Spirit's sanctuary. We've heard that so many times that we seldom think about what it truly means. God's Spirit lives inside us! He has chosen our flesh and blood as the place from which He shines. And not only that—Christ died on the cross so that nothing would stand in the way of God's Spirit within us.

When we consider all that, why would we want to do anything that would dim the Spirit's light? Abusing drugs is dangerous to both our bodies and our spirits. God wants both to shine with His light.

Jesus, You make all things new, including me. Thank You for Your Spirit in me, guiding me, teaching me Your truth, and stepping up for me in prayer (Romans 8:26–27). I see my drug abuse for the rebellion against You that it is. I see now that I chose darkness instead of Your light for too long. I need Your light now to push the drugs out of my system, and I need You to give me the desire to take them out of my mind.

◇◇◇

Lord, keep me sober. One day at a time. One hour at a time. I know that my body is not my own. I was created by You and for You. Help me to honor You with my body. Give me the strength I need to turn away from drugs.

◇◇◇

God, You are not trying to keep me from having a good time. Help me to realize that the "good times" I've been chasing aren't good for me at all. Renew my heart and help me to want the things that are good for me. Drugs are repulsive. Why do I keep going back to them? Help me, God, before it's too late.

◇◇◇

Lord, keep me sober-minded and on my guard. I know that the enemy of my soul prowls around like a hungry lion, looking to eat me alive. I believe that if I can stand firm, You will make me whole and strong. (1 Peter 5:8–11)

◇◇◇

God, I know You're not a goody-goody! You don't make rules simply for the sake of making them. In fact, I can say along with the apostle Paul, "I am allowed to do anything" (1 Corinthians 6:12 NLT). But even though all things are allowed, not everything is helpful or productive. I refuse to be enslaved by anything.

Jesus, in You I am free. Help me to use that freedom in productive ways. I want to make a difference in the world. Drugs cause me to be selfish. I want to learn to be selfless. Heal me from this dependence. I want to be used for Your kingdom.

◇◇◇

God, You have called me to be salt and light to Your world. When I'm abusing drugs, I can't be either of these. I want my conversations to be seasoned with fervor for You. I want to shine as a light for You in the dark places of this world.

◇◇◇

Lord God, I am humbled that You lowered Yourself to my level to show me how much You love me. You have been with me in some very dark places and times, and I owe You everything. I trust the timing of Your deliverance from my addiction to drugs.

◇◇◇

Lord, I know Your voice. Help me to tune into the voice of my Master, my Good Shepherd (John 10:27), not the other voices that call to me. The world is full of pleasures that wind up as disasters. There's a new promise for a greater high or escape every day in the places I've been living. Help me to escape this dangerous obstacle course and exchange it for the straight paths You've prepared for me.

◇◇◇

God, I don't want sin to reign over me. You are my King, not drugs. Bring me back from the dead. Make me alive again in my faith and in my walk with You as Savior and Lord of my life. I want to be Your instrument of righteousness (Romans 6:12–14).

Create in me a clean heart, God,
and renew in me a steadfast spirit (Psalm 51:10).

◇◇◇

Jesus, You called me to freedom. I don't want to use
that freedom for something that will lead me away from
You. Instead, help me to always use Your freedom
to serve others. (Galatians 5:13)

◇◇◇

Creator God, You want me to be this world's "salt." You have
called me to be a light. Drug abuse robs my salt of its savor.
It knocks my light off its stand and instead, it puts a bushel over
it, so that no one can see it. Make me truly "salty," God! Let my
light shine so that everyone can see it. Be glorified in me.
Don't let me do anything that will get in
the way of that. (Matthew 5:13–16)

◇◇◇

God, set me free from the fear and anger that drove me to a
life of drug addiction. I have been consumed with a burning
need for drugs at different times, and I've made compromises,
excuses, and mistakes that have hurt me and others—and that
have separated me from my family, friends, and You. Deliver me
from the false acceptance of my addiction as insurmountable.
Nothing is impossible for You (Matthew 19:26). I need You,
God, and You alone can save me. Forgive me, heal me, and lead
me to the help and support I need to fight my addiction.

Father, I know You want me to be healthy and whole. But I also know that the devil is after me, like a lion on the prowl (1 Peter 5:8–11). I commit to standing firm against my addiction, to being on the alert for warning signs, and to giving You all my worries and troubles. Set my feet on Your firm foundation.

◇◇◇

Lord, I give myself to You. Help me to do my best to be a worker who needs not be ashamed of anything, someone who does a good job handling Your truth (2 Timothy 2:15). I refuse to let drugs get in the way between us!

◇◇◇

God, don't let sin reign in my flesh, in the form of drugs or anything else. I don't want to obey anything that has to do with sin. I don't want my body to be used for anything but Your righteousness. I give myself to You; in fact, I give You my entire body to use as Your instrument. I don't want sin to have any dominion over me, for I know that Your grace is mine. (Romans 6:12–14)

◇◇◇

Create in me a clean heart, loving Lord, and renew in me a steadfast spirit (Psalm 51:10).

DYSFUNCTIONAL RELATIONSHIPS

No one came with me. Everyone abandoned me. . . .
But the Lord stood with me and gave me strength.

2 TIMOTHY 4:16–17 NLT

◆

It's hard to cope with relationships that are broken. We keep hoping that somehow things will change. That in spite of the way things have always gone in the past, *this time* things will be different.

We play our own role in these dysfunctional relationships. We may be what counselors call an enabler, allowing the individuals involved to keep on doing things that hurt. Or we may get sucked into the fights and the insults, the nonproductive conversations and the hurtful habits.

But God wants to heal our entire lives, including our relationships. This healing is not likely to happen overnight—but our God can do amazing things. A miracle that takes time is still a miracle!

Lord, You know I grew up in a very messed-up family. There was no emotional or spiritual balance, starting with my parents. We were a case study for Proverbs 11:29 (MSG): "Exploit or abuse your family, and end up with a fistful of air; common sense tells you it's a stupid way to live." I'm starting to see some of the same patterns in my own family, though I swore it would be different. I want it to be different. Help me identify where the problems are, and then help me take steps to create a mature, responsible, healthy set of relationships. Bring me people who can teach me differently and hold me accountable.

◇◇◇

God, some of this is not my fault. Help me to see the parts I do need to take responsibility for and make the necessary changes. I want this relationship to be better, and yet I keep doing and saying the same things. Wanting is not enough. I must take action. Guide me, I pray, and help me to see my part in it all so that I can change it.

◇◇◇

Give me a new heart, God. I need one. I'm so angry and hurt, and I try to control this relationship but I always fail. You are the only way, truth, and life. Please renew my efforts today and give me a brand-new heart toward the people involved (Psalm 51:10).

◇◇◇

Creator God, I focus so often on how I want others to change. I pray for them, I nag them, I lecture them, I beg them, I try to manipulate them. Ultimately, none of it does much good. Instead, God, show me where I need to change. I put myself into Your hands. I'm willing to have You do whatever it takes to heal my relationships.

When my kids are disrespectful, I respond with anger and harsh
words. I know my anger doesn't accomplish Your purposes in
any of our lives (James 1:20). Forgive me, help me to forgive my
children, and let their hearts be forgiving toward me. I need to
focus on bringing them up "in the discipline and instruction
of the Lord" (Ephesians 6:4 ESV). I know that kind of discipline
begins with me showing self-control and wisdom that
comes from knowing You better.

◇◇◇

Heavenly Father, I hear about boundaries, but I don't even know
what they would look like in my world. I'm constantly doing
everything for everyone, trying to please, trying to keep the
peace. I know this isn't healthy. Teach me where I need
to establish healthy boundaries, Father. Give me the opportunity
to take care of myself so that I can have something
left over to give to others.

◇◇◇

God, I heard it said once that you won't get a different result if
you keep doing the same things over and over again. I feel like
I'm caught in a bad dream. My loved one and I keep having the
same issues, the same fights, the same dysfunction between us.
Please give me discernment so that I might see a new way.
I'm tired of these same old results.

◇◇◇

Dear Father, I feel selfish and guilty taking time for myself.
I long to run away—but I'm afraid of what I'll find when I
come back. Remind me that I'm no use to anyone if I
don't take care of myself. Give me the courage to
set boundaries that protect my own well-being.

Jesus, I need help. I need a counselor or someone really wise to guide me. I don't know whom I can trust and who can give me sound, biblical advice. Please show me where to turn so that I don't have to bear this alone any longer.
This relationship is destroying my life.

◇◇◇

God, I can't admit this to my parents or siblings. There is not a single friend I feel that I can turn to with the depth of this dysfunction in my marriage. I'm embarrassed. I didn't know it could get this bad. I had no idea when we took our vows how hard it would be for me to keep them. Please help me. Show me someone I can trust who can help us through this. Things have to improve, and I believe they can. . .with Your help.

◇◇◇

Father, the dynamic in my family seems out of control. I feel powerless to change the lack of harmony between me and my spouse, the foolishness my kids seem committed to, and the difficulties of getting along with other family members. But then I think of Your purposes in all of that. Sin has cut us off from You and led to relationships driven by selfishness. We need a Savior. Fortunately, in Jesus Christ, You gave us what we needed most and deserved least—grace, forgiveness, and hope.
Let me lead my family in an ongoing experience of the grace and love that starts with You.

Jesus, I need help. I can't cope with this relationship on my own any longer. I need a counselor, a friend, a support group—something! Someone who will understand what I'm going through, Someone who can give me advice. Please help me find the right person, the person who will reveal Your light and wisdom to me.

◇◇◇

God, I am struggling to change painful, repeated, dysfunctional behavior in my family. Help me see what I need to see—the patterns that need to change, both in me and in others. Guide me in taking steps toward healing and consistently healthy behavior for all of us, and lead me in finding resources and people who can advise me and hold me accountable. I am reminded that Your "divine power has given us everything we need for a godly life" (2 Peter 1:3 NIV).

◇◇◇

Lord, I need Your help getting away from a toxic relationship. Somehow, I ended up partnering with someone who is consistently negative, unethical, and generally miserable. I feel like I'm endorsing this person's attitudes and actions just by being in the same room. Please show me if there is something I have done to contribute to the behavior, so I can try to make it right. Otherwise, give me the courage to speak up, and even to get out, before this person's problems poison my thinking and behavior.

ELDERLY PARENTS

*Listen with respect to the father who raised you,
and when your mother grows old, don't neglect her.*
PROVERBS 23:22 MSG

The scripture makes clear that we owe a debt of love and responsibility to our parents as they grow older. It may not always be an easy debt to fill. After all, our lives are already busy, filled with responsibilities to family and home, career and community. Our parents' growing needs seldom come at a time that's convenient for us. Instead, the season of life when we're the busiest with our own families and lives, doing our best to juggle all of life's growing demands, is the very time when our parents are likely to need more of our time and attention.

We may be surprised, though, to find that as our parents age, our changed relationship with them has its rewards as well. Our parents are not too old to offer us love and advice, if we can open our hearts to them. God will bless us through them—sometimes in surprising ways!

Father, as my parents get older, I need to be more deliberate about spending time with them. I don't want to get so busy that I neglect the people who brought me into the world. Life is so busy, but I know I must make time for what matters most to me.

◇◇◇

God, my parents are in a season of life where it's easy for them to become isolated. Bless them with good relationships and enjoyable social connections. Give them good health— sound minds and bodies, despite the rigors of age. Keep them connected to You, and help them to finish strong in walking with You and advancing Your kingdom.

◇◇◇

God, You knit my parents together in their mothers' wombs. You have been with them all of their lives. I know You will remain faithful through this life and the next to keep Your promises to them. Thank You for their long lives and the blessing that my mom and dad are to me.

◇◇◇

Father, it's not always easy to know what to do. I want my parents to enjoy independence as long as they possibly can. But I'm scared when things happen that could prove unsafe for them. As I make tough decisions for my elderly parents, please guide me and give me wisdom.

◇◇◇

Loving Lord, I pray that You will be with my parents. I know You were with them before I was ever born. You were there when they were babies, and You are with them now in their old age. You will continue to carry them. You made them, and You will always be with them. (Isaiah 46:3–4)

Jesus, You—who came to us directly from the Father—were willing to serve us. You even washed Your disciples' feet. Make me able and willing to follow Your example now and serve my parents, in whatever ways they need me.

◇◇◇

Jesus, You were a servant leader who even washed Your disciples' feet. Please give me a servant's heart too. If I need to help my parents with things like bathing or going to the restroom, allow me to know how to assist while helping them feel okay about it. I want them to have their dignity. I love them so.

◇◇◇

Gray hair is a crown of glory, which is gained by living a godly life (Proverbs 16:31). Help me to remember to honor my parents to their very last days. They have earned and deserve my respect.

◇◇◇

God, use me to bless my parents. And let me be open to Your blessing coming to me through them.

◇◇◇

Father, I pray that You will give my parents moments of brightness today. Even as their bodies are beginning to fail them, I know that You remain faithful and true. Give them neighbors who care and joyful moments such as watching birds out their kitchen window. . .just little things to cheer them through the day. Thank You, Lord, for loving my mom and dad.

◇◇◇

Even in the Old Testament, You made sure the people knew that they were to respect the elderly. Your law told them to stand up in the presence of their elders (Leviticus 19:32). I'm so thankful for my parents, and I want to show them the respect they are due.

Heavenly Father, may my parents flourish like tall
trees planted in Your house. May they still bear fruit,
even intheir old age. Give them spirits that are ever
young and growing. (Psalm 92:12–14)

◇◇◇

Lord, Your Word makes it clear that I owe my parents a portion
of my love, time, and care as they grow older. I commit myself
to treating them with the respect and consideration I will want
from my own children in my latter years. It's a privilege
to care for them, and I want to do it well.

◇◇◇

God, give me ears to hear my parents' wisdom, even when it lies
hidden beneath dementia or illness. May I honor them with
love, as they have honored me. Let me give back to them from
the wealth they gave me when I was young. Fill their
old age with joy and peace.

◇◇◇

You know how busy I am, Lord. It's hard for me to sort out the
demands on my time. Show me what my priorities should be.
Give me wisdom to know how to help my parents as they age.

◇◇◇

God, it's hard to think of my parents getting older,
growing frail, and getting sick. I'm not sure I'm ready for this
transition to caring for them the way they cared for me as a kid.
Prepare me for the coming changes. Guide me in having these
hard conversations with them about what to do in a crisis,
and help me to listen well and figure out how to help.

EMOTIONAL AND SPIRITUAL PAIN

But the God of all grace, who hath called us unto his eternal glory by Christ Jesus, after that ye have suffered a while, make you perfect, stablish, strengthen, settle you.

1 PETER 5:10 KJV

Emotional and spiritual pain fills us with fear. It breaks our hearts. It robs us of our normal daily joys. These emotions don't mean that our faith has failed, though. The Gospels make clear that Jesus suffered as much emotionally in the garden, praying before His death, as He did physically when He was actually hanging from the cross. If Jesus could not escape this anguish, then we should not expect to either. Instead of fighting our emotions, trying to wrestle them into submission, we can surrender them into God's hands to do with them as He wills. Ultimately, this pain will not make us weak—instead, it will make us stronger!

Lord, You know all that I'm feeling right now. My heart hurts, and my spirit feels weak and wobbly. Remind me, Lord, that I am Your child, and even this emotional pain comes to me through Your loving hand. This hurts so much—but I believe that down the road a ways, I will reap a harvest of peace and righteousness from what I'm experiencing now (Hebrews 12:11).

◇◇◇

I know, Jesus, that when You walked on the earth, You too felt the strain of emotional torment. Come beside me now, I ask, and lead me through this time when emotional strength is too weak to cope. Help me to find peace and calm in Your presence.

◇◇◇

Remind me, Holy Spirit, that this temporary suffering is producing in me an everlasting weight of glory, far beyond any comparison. Teach me to focus less on feelings and more on that which I can't perceive right now with my emotions. Be more real to me, I pray, than any pain (2 Corinthians 4:17–18).

◇◇◇

God, You promised to wipe every tear from our eyes, because one day there will be no more death or sorrow or crying or pain. All these things will be gone forever (Revelation 21:4). When my emotions overwhelm me, remind me of that promise.

EMOTIONAL AND SPIRITUAL WEAKNESS

"My grace is all you need. My power works best in weakness."
2 CORINTHIANS 12:9 NLT

When we feel as though we're too weak to accomplish anything, we often feel blue and depressed. Our physical weakness makes us feel equally weak emotionally and spiritually. Our self-concepts suffer. We measure ourselves against what we used to be, and we come up lacking.

But it doesn't have to be that way. When we stop focusing on our own lack and instead turn our eyes to God, He has a chance to reveal His mighty power. His grace will be revealed in our lives. In fact, we may experience His grace and strength in new ways, more powerfully than ever before.

I am so weak, God. But You promised me that Your power is made perfect in weakness, that Your grace is all I need. Here, God. I put my weakness in Your hands. Use it however You want. May Your grace fill my life.

◇◇◇

I'm tired of being sick, Lord. The challenge is too big for me. My self-confidence fails. I can't help but compare how big the challenge is to my meager abilities for confronting it. My faith wavers. Help me.

◇◇◇

Jesus, I believe I can do all things—because You make me strong (Philippians 4:13).

◇◇◇

I know, dear Jesus, that when I admit how weak I truly am, then You have the chance to reveal Your strength. The challenge that lies ahead shrinks when I compare it to Your immensity. Keep me focused on You and Your power.

◇◇◇

Therefore, Christ, I'll be content with weakness and distresses and difficulties, for Your sake; for I know that when I am weak, then I am strong—because of You (2 Corinthians 12:10).

◇◇◇

Father, You give strength to the weary, and when we lack strength, You give us power. Though young people with their strong, healthy bodies get tired and stumble, I will have new strength to keep going—because I am waiting only for You. (Isaiah 40:29–31)

ENEMIES

"I'm telling you to love your enemies. Let them bring out the best in you, not the worst. When someone gives you a hard time, respond with the energies of prayer, for then you are working out of your true selves, your God-created selves. This is what God does. He gives his best—the sun to warm and the rain to nourish—to everyone, regardless.... In a word, what I'm saying is, Grow up. You're kingdom subjects. Now live like it. Live out your God-created identity. Live generously and graciously toward others, the way God lives toward you."

MATTHEW 5:44–48 MSG

Sometimes Christians ignore what Jesus says here in the Gospel of Matthew. We make enemies out of the people we don't approve of, the people who disagree with what we believe, who have different politics, different values, different agendas. We might deny that we treat them like enemies—but do we act as though we love them? Do we give them our best? Do we pray for them with all our energy? And if we do pray for them, are we only praying that they will change their minds and think like we do—or are we truly praying that God will bless them, regardless?

Jesus tells us that we can't be His mature followers—in fact, we can't even realize our own God-given identities—if we don't start treating everyone, including our enemies, with the same grace and generosity God has shown us.

Lord, I realize I've been harboring grudges in my heart—making enemies simply by failing to love people the way You've called me to. I can think of people who are not loving me—not looking out for my best interests or being only for themselves—but this is where the rubber meets the road, isn't it? This is where I can stump the world and show the difference You make in my life. But I can't do it without You. Forgive me for my hardheartedness and give me Your heart, Lord.

◇◇◇

Jesus, help me to fight evil with good. Give me the strength to take a deep breath and show love even to those who are not easy to love. I read about how You asked the Father to forgive those who crucified You. That's unbelievable to me, and yet, I'm called to love and pray for my enemies as well. Help me, I pray.

◇◇◇

Heavenly Father, I pray right now in this moment for the ones who have hurt me. I lift them up by name before Your throne. Perhaps they truly "know not what they do." I know that hurt people are known to hurt people. Please heal the wounds in their souls. Please use me as a representative of Your grace and generosity.

◇◇◇

Dear Jesus, help me to follow Your example always. Let me not work to get even with those who have hurt me. Remind me that if I seek revenge, I am only multiplying the evil in this world. Instead, help me to love.

◇◇◇

Lord, bless this person who hurt me so badly. Do good in his life. Be with the person who disagrees with me. Bring good things to her. I ask that Your love would shine in their lives.

Jesus, my real enemies are the flesh, the world, and the devil—
and You have overcome all of them (1 John 4:4). Everyone
needs You, and even though some deliberately set themselves
against You, I can stand against their words and behavior and
still show them a better way. I can still pray for their salvation,
still obey You when You tell me, "Do not be overcome by evil,
but overcome evil with good" (Romans 12:21 NKJV).

◇◇◇

God, I'm so quick to defend myself sometimes. The tongue-
in-cheek comment or sarcastic remark that comes my way
from a coworker is rarely ignored. Often, I retaliate. I am
quick to speak. The comebacks fly! Take control over my quick
tongue, Father. I pray that I will stop and think before I speak.
Sometimes saying nothing is far more powerful.

◇◇◇

Holy Spirit, be my Comforter. I've been wounded by someone
who really knows the buttons to push. I'm filled with hate and,
in my own strength, I'm unable to muster up love for this
individual. I need You to be strong in my weakness.
Replace my anger with compassion.

◇◇◇

Help me, Jesus, to consider this person's perspective and
the hurt within that must drive these careless wounds he
inflicts on others. I pray for healing in his heart.

◇◇◇

Holy Spirit, fill me with Your love. Help me to not only love
You but all those whom You have created. Teach me not to be
so sensitive to slights and insults. Help me to focus always
on what is good for others, rather than myself.
Teach me to love as You love.

God, You alone know all things—including the true intentions and thoughts of every person. I don't know why this person treated me the way he did; I only know the effects. It hurts and angers me, but I am in no position to judge. So, if it's possible, I want to understand this person better. Even though I don't like him, I know You sent Jesus to die for him. This person matters to You, and so, he matters to me.

◇◇◇

You emphasized a lot of things in Your teachings, Jesus, but the greatest was love. Love is a powerful force capable of changing a heart. Your love changed my heart. Use me, I pray, to be a living example of unconditional love to others today—especially those who are my enemies.

◇◇◇

You are the God of the impossible, Lord. You are the maker of every heart. You have the power to soften hearts and turn enemies into fast friends. Be a miracle worker in this situation, I pray.

◇◇◇

I want to be more like You, Jesus. Amazingly, You treated Your enemies with respect. You loved them. May I not be overcome by evil, but instead, by the power of Your Spirit, may I overcome evil with good (Romans 12:21).

◇◇◇

Lord, if I only treat well those I agree with, those who are kind to me, those who love me, then I'm not showing the world Your love. Help me to love those who disagree with me, those who are unkind, those who are filled with hate. Use me to spread peace and love throughout the world.

God, make me willing to open my heart to those people I don't like. Turn my enemies into friends. You have power to transform all relationships. Do what seems impossible. Bring harmony and friendship to my world.

◇◇◇

God, You know how angry I feel right now with this person. Show me their perspective. You know how hurt I am. Reveal to me the ways I have hurt them. You know I am filled with hate. Turn my hate into Your love.

◇◇◇

I'm struggling to love my enemies, God. The emotions their behavior stirs up in me are powerful—desires to pay them back in kind, fighting fire with fire, placing blame. But while they have been overwhelmed by their emotions, I will not be overcome by mine. If I treat them the way they've treated me, evil wins. I'd be sinking to their level instead of rising to Yours. It's taking all I have not to hit below the belt in my words and actions, but I need Your Spirit to help me go lower—in humility and love and grace. Let Your love in me produce repentance in them.

◇◇◇

Father, You've told me not to avenge myself—that You will repay those who have wronged me (Romans 12:19). But You've also told me to go beyond that, not just to avoid seeking revenge but to feed a hungry enemy or give a thirsty one a drink, "for by so doing you will heap burning coals on his head" (v. 20 ESV). I admit that the image tickles my vengeful thoughts—forgive me, please—but I realize that You're not talking about returning an injury but snuffing out whatever impulses drove their behavior. By being kind instead of mean, I can kindle the possibility of forgiveness and reconciliation.

FACING DEATH

" 'Well done, my good and faithful servant. . . . Let's celebrate together!' "
MATTHEW 25:21 NLT

We fear the unknown—and death is the greatest unknown there is. As Christians, we say we believe in the resurrection of the dead, but deep in our hearts, we wonder what that means. The closer death comes to us, the harder it may be for us to hold on to our confidence in eternal life. And when death starts breathing down our necks—as we grow older or if we face a terminal illness—we are forced to confront our doubts head-on. Is there really anything beyond death? Or will all that we are cease to exist once we stop breathing?

The Bible assures us that physical death is not the end. Jesus came to this earth so that our fears could be put to rest. He has promised us that He has prepared a place for us in the life to come—and when we die, we will hear His voice welcoming us into the eternal celebration.

Lord, the journey to the end is hard. I thought I would read the
Bible more, pray more, minister more—really make whatever
time I had left a final tour de force for Your glory. Instead,
I find myself weakened, unable to concentrate long enough to
read more than a few verses or utter a few words. Even though I
am on the way to becoming so much more than I ever was,
I feel like I am so much less. My hope is that my reliance on
You for everything is reaching its fullness—that You
will somehow shine that much brighter in my
growing weakness (2 Corinthians 12:9).

◇◇◇

God, I'm trying to accept what lies ahead. But I have to tell
You, death is no friend of mine! This isn't what I want. It feels
unnatural. It feels wrong. I'm glad that Your Son felt the same
way about it. He prayed for a way around death, if there was any
way possible. And I'm glad Your scripture refers to death as
the "last enemy" (1 Corinthians 15:26). I like knowing that
You and I are in this together. Death is not natural. It's not
what You intended. You created me to live
forever. And because of Jesus, I will.

◇◇◇

God, it's easy to say one doesn't fear death—until it's knocking
at the door. I know I am drawing closer and closer to the time
when I will take my final breath. Please reassure me that while
death is "the final enemy" (1 Corinthians 15:26), You have
already defeated it! I will live forever with You in heaven.

Heavenly Father, I entrust my family and friends into Your care.
For so long, I've worked and tried to care for them. I've given
all that I can. My time draws near. Please take care of
them for me as I have to leave them behind.

◇◇◇

Jesus, be with those I love and have to leave behind.
I surrender them into Your loving arms. I know You
will be with them even when I no longer can be.

◇◇◇

Father, I can't wait to see You, but the thought of going through
death's door is still daunting. I know my fear of the unknown
is a remnant of this sin-broken body, but I want to maintain
the right balance of loss and hope in the time I have left.
My gain will mean loss for my loved ones, and I ask You
to comfort them and give them Your peace,
now and then. Give us all Your peace.

◇◇◇

Jesus, I'm thinking about Paul's words, "To live is Christ,
and to die is gain" (Philippians 1:21 NKJV). I won't embrace
death because You can still use my life as a witness to make
Your name greater. Still, I am grieving now, if only
because my absence will make my loved ones sad.

◇◇◇

Lord, I feel so lonely. I don't want to burden the people I love
with my feelings. I know they're dealing with my approaching
death in their own way. They can't help me with what I'm
facing. I'm all alone. Thank You that You're here with me.
I'm counting on You in a way I never have before.

The valley of the shadow of death never seemed so real as it
does today. I will not fear it. You are here with me, just as
You promised to be. You protect me. You comfort me.
I will live forever in the house of my Lord (Psalm 23).

◇◇◇

I am fully known. You put me together in my mother's womb.
But I have walked through this life with only a glimpse of
who You are. My humanity has kept me from knowing fully.
There are secret things that simply cannot be understood in
this life. I'm coming close to the time when I will know!
I will know fully just as I am fully known. I look
forward to that, Lord (1 Corinthians 13:12)!

◇◇◇

All my life, I've been looking at a dim reflection of You in a
poor mirror, Lord, catching cloudy glimpses of who You are.
Pretty soon, though, I'm going to see You face to face,
with perfect clarity. I'll know You completely,
just as You know me. (1 Corinthians 13:12)

◇◇◇

Jesus, even though I'm walking through the valley of the shadow
of death, I'm not afraid. I know You are with me. You protect
and comfort me. You're setting the table for me, a place
where I can sit down and be nourished, right here in death's
presence. Your goodness and mercy follow me wherever I go,
and I know I will live forever with You. (Psalm 23:4–6)

◇◇◇

You died, Jesus. You died upon the cross. You died, just as I am
dying here in this place now. You took a final breath, just as
I will soon. But hallelujah, You did not stay in the grave!

I am in the garden, Jesus. I'm praying for another way.
I'm asking my Father that the cup might pass, that I might not
have to drink the bitterness of death. But my body fails me,
and I grow weaker. I know deep down that He is going to take
me home soon. Give me the acceptance that You had when
You realized Your death was not an option but a certainty.
I want to go in peace to my eternal home.

◇◇◇

God, there's no formula for facing my death, but let me find
strength in Your Word: "None of us lives to himself, and none
of us dies to himself. For if we live, we live to the Lord,
and if we die, we die to the Lord" (Romans 14:7–8 ESV).
Come what may, I am Yours, Father.

◇◇◇

Jesus, when I read about Your death on the cross, I can
tell You went through much of what I'm experiencing now.
You felt lonely and forsaken. You wondered where God was.
You felt death's pain and horror. And yet in the midst of all
that, You still trusted Your Father. You put Your spirit in
His hands. God, I want to follow Your Son's example.
I commit my spirit into Your hands.

◇◇◇

Jesus, You endured death because You had Your eyes on the joy
that lies ahead (Hebrews 12:2). Give me a glimpse of that same
joy. May it be my focal point, even in the midst of pain and fear.

Death brings change, Lord. There's no way around it. I've been affected by others' deaths, so it's not pride that makes me say that my death will affect other people. Their new normal will be harder than mine, though. I'll be with You—no more pain or sorrow—but they'll still be here, missing me and waiting for You. I confess, it makes me sad. All I can do is love them while I am here and trust them to Your good care.

◇◇◇

I'm looking to Job's words for comfort today, Father: "Set a date when you'll see me again. If we humans die, will we live again? That's my question. All through these difficult days I keep hoping, waiting for the final change—for resurrection! Homesick with longing for the creature you made, you'll call—and I'll answer! You'll watch over every step I take, but you won't keep track of my missteps. My sins will be stuffed in a sack and thrown into the sea—sunk in deep ocean" (Job 14:13–17 MSG). We'll be together, and You'll give me a new, perfect version of my body, just as You did with Jesus (1 Corinthians 15). This one's getting pretty busted and worn out, so thank You, Father.

FAILURE

Can anything ever separate us from Christ's love? Does it mean he no longer loves us if we have trouble or calamity, or are persecuted, or hungry, or destitute, or in danger, or threatened with death? . . . No, despite all these things, overwhelming victory is ours through Christ, who loved us.

ROMANS 8:35, 37 NLT

We all want to be successful. Countless books have been written on the topic, offering us yet another secret formula for guaranteeing that success will be ours. But the reality is this: we all experience failures. Theodore Roosevelt once said something along these lines: "The only person who never makes a mistake [who never experiences failure] is the person who never does anything."

Even the great heroes of our Christian faith experienced their share of failure. Abraham and Moses, Elijah and David, Peter and Paul—they all knew what it was like to make serious mistakes. But God used even their failures to bring them to the place where He wanted them to be.

And He will do the same for us. No matter how many times we fail, His love never does. And in the midst of our failures, we can still find victory in Christ.

God, I confess that it's my ego that gets bruised when I fail.
It's a reminder that I'm still striving for self-sufficiency,
for some sort of merit apart from my value to You. Forgive me.
Let my real accomplishments be measured in relationships,
beginning with my relationship with You.

◇◇◇

I want to be successful. Who doesn't? I want to do well in my
career and climb the ladder. I want to be a good friend and
coworker. And yet, I fail. I let people down. I miss deadlines.
I come up short. Remind me that You love me not
one bit less when I fail than when I am victorious.
Thank You for Your unconditional love, God.

◇◇◇

My failure leads me to repentance. I come to You when I fail.
I seek You. When You say You work all things together for
good for those who love You, I think that includes our failures.
If I were always a winner, I would not rely on You as much.
I fall into Your arms when I fail. You are
always there, steadfast and true.

◇◇◇

Loving Lord, You know I long to be a success. I want to live the
victorious Christian life. I want to please You. I want others to
be impressed with my faith. I want to be the person You created.
I know my motives are all mixed up—but I do sincerely want to
follow You. And yet again and again, I fail. I let You down. I let
others down. I let myself down. Teach me, Lord, to find You
even in the midst of failure. Let me never put off holding out
my arms to You, so that You can pick me up and put me back
on my feet. Thank You that Your grace never fails.

Sometimes I refuse to try because I'm afraid I'll fail. I did this as a child and I thought I would outgrow it, but I haven't. Instead of avoiding a sport or activity, I now avoid bigger things—like relationships and job applications. Give me confidence, Father, and strengthen my spirit so that it's okay even if I do fail.

◇◇◇

My identity is in Christ Jesus. I am saved and loved and cherished. My identity does not depend on how well I do things. Remind me of this, Father. Thank You for loving me so unconditionally.

◇◇◇

God, Peter denied three times in one night that he even knew You. I would call that a failure. And yet, You still used him. You understood His humanity. Use me too, I pray, in spite of my weakness and failures.

◇◇◇

I'm trying to remember that You are good, that You work all things together for good for those who love You. It's hard for me to think that Your will for my life could include failure—that there are things I could never learn from You through success. But here we are. I will trust You, Lord, even in this. Teach me.

◇◇◇

Use my failures to help me improve, Lord Jesus. When I yell at my children, use this to teach me patience next time. When I miss a deadline at work, teach me to prioritize better in the future. I can improve. Help me to have the confidence I need to do better next time.

The world may call me a failure, but You see it quite differently, Lord. I'm in this world, but I'm not of it. I'm an alien here, for my real home is heaven. When I don't have the largest bank account because I've given freely to others, remind me that money is not the most important thing. When I choose to stay in a place where I'm making an impact for the kingdom, remind me that this honors You. It's okay to let an opportunity for promotion or change pass by if I'm where I feel I should be. In Jesus' name I pray for confidence to do what's right regardless of how the world may view it.

◇◇◇

Sometimes, Jesus, I feel so afraid of failure that I can't seem to do anything at all. I don't even want to try something in case I won't be successful. My fear paralyzes me. Christ Jesus, release me from my fear, I pray. Remind me not to take myself so seriously. Help me to see that the world won't end if I fail. Give me joy in the effort, whatever the results.

◇◇◇

Even though my efforts often fail, Lord,
help me to remember that I am never a failure.
My worth is safe, for it comes from You.

◇◇◇

God, Abraham failed You when he fled to Egypt during the drought. Moses lost his temper and turned to violence more than once. David committed both adultery and murder. Peter denied Your Son. And yet You used all the people who failed You so badly. Use me too.

Father, help me figure out what kind of failure this is—a moral, spiritual failure on my part, or a defeat that has nothing to do with my walk with You. I'm not feeling particularly brave or ambitious at this point, but I am willing to deal with whatever You show me. If it's sin, I will confess it and turn from it. If it's something You're allowing me to face, I will try my best to learn what You're trying to teach me—and to remember that my priority in life is to know You better. You decide the measure of my success, not me.

◇◇◇

Help me to learn from my failures, loving Lord. Use them to help me grow.

◇◇◇

Remind me, Jesus, that sometimes what the world considers failure is not failure at all from eternity's perspective. After all, Your disciples must have assumed at first that Your death on the cross was the worst failure of all. And yet what looked like failure brought new life to all creation.

◇◇◇

God, I am trying to learn from my failure. What are You trying to develop in me? What character trait or spiritual gift or story are You building in me to use to connect with someone later? I want to be like Joshua and Caleb when they went with ten other guys to spy out Canaan. The ten all saw the giants living in the land, but only Joshua and Caleb said, "Let us go up at once and take possession, for we are well able to overcome it" (Numbers 13:30 NKJV). My only true failure would be in giving up. I will hope in You as I try again.

FAMILY FEUDS

"The Sun of Righteousness will rise with healing in his wings. And you will go free."
MALACHI 4:2 NLT

Do you dread family get-togethers? Are holidays occasions for conflict? Do long-standing family feuds mar what should be happy family times?

We're not talking about the McCoys and the Hatfields here, or the Capulets and Montagues, fights between *different* families; we're talking about intrafamily feuds, the kind between aunts and uncles, between sisters and brothers, or between grandparents and parents. These are the painful conflicts that continue year after year. Maybe they lurk beneath the surface, bursting out unexpectedly over some small issue. Or maybe they're expressed in icy silence that's never broken. Maybe you wish everyone would just grow up. Or maybe you're a part of the feud.

God longs to bring His love to your family's life. His Spirit is waiting to seep into the cracks in the anger, to water the hurt feelings with healing, to slowly bring new life to what has been broken for so long. Will you open your own heart to let the process begin? God longs to heal you and set you free.

God, I confess that I'm guilty of judging my problem relative.
I've taken the differences in our beliefs and lifestyles and
somewhere in my heart decided that I'm a better person.
Like Paul wrote, "Why do you pass judgment on your brother?
Or you, why do you despise your brother? For we will all stand
before the judgment seat of God" (Romans 14:10 ESV).
You've forgiven me, and I know I need to be more forgiving,
even if my relative doesn't think they need to be forgiven,
so that I don't become bitter in my words and actions.

◇◇◇

You offer a peace that the world simply cannot. It's a peace that
comes only through a personal walk with Your Son, Jesus.
It's a peace that my family needs desperately. Please bless us
with a peace that passes all understanding. I ask this
in the powerful name of Jesus.

◇◇◇

Please help us turn our barriers into bridges. Please help us to
consider the others' perspectives. God, I ask You to please
heal our wounds. Bind them up. Change us from
the inside out. We need You, Lord.

◇◇◇

Dear Father, the whole world is crying out for peace—peace
between nations and even peace within homes. We long for
peace in our family as well, the kind of peace that comes from
walking in step with one another and with You. Help us to learn
the laws of peace and how to foster harmony in
our family through Your Word.

Find my broken family useful to Your kingdom, God. Cause us to consider how much better our passion would be spent on spreading the Gospel rather than feuding among ourselves. We've been angry for so long that I'm not sure any of us even remember how it all began. Forgive us, God. Change us. Use us, I pray.

◇◇◇

Bring peace to my family, Lord. Heal our ancient wounds. Build bridges between us. May we find the way to love each other again.

◇◇◇

Father, there's a person in our family whose attitudes and behavior constantly causes conflict. I want to do something about it, but I want to do it the right way. I want to be a peacemaker, and I want to have Your heart of forgiveness and reconciliation and Your desire to pursue truth and purity. I don't want to address someone else's speck if I have a log in my eye (Matthew 7:5). Let me see myself clearly, and then guide me in approaching this person with a clean heart.

◇◇◇

Jesus, my own family has hurt me so deeply. I don't feel like forgiving, but I know it's Your command. I know that I should forgive seventy times seven times. I know that I cannot be healed unless this war within my family comes to a halt. Please guide me in how to help that happen. It needs to happen soon, Lord.

◇◇◇

God, help me to place You above my family. Family is important, but I know that You are more important still. When I cease to find my worth in what my relatives think of me, perhaps I'll be freed up to love them and forgive them for the ways they've hurt me. Help me to find my identity in You.

God, when I read the Old Testament, I realize You know all
about flawed families. Jacob and Rebekah plotted for Isaac's
favor. Joseph's brothers sold him into slavery. David's own
son conspired to murder him. And yet You used these broken
families. Countless generations have learned of You from their
stories, and from their genetic line Your Son was born.
Father, I pray that You would use my family too, despite
its flaws. Shed Your grace over us. Transform us.

◇◇◇

Jesus, I'm trying to practice Your attitude as I seek the best
interests of someone in my family who makes my life hard
(Philippians 2:4–5). I'm hoping that doing so will help me see
the obstacles this person presents as opportunities to show
Your love and the difference grace makes.

◇◇◇

Jesus, how can I love these people who have hurt me so deeply?
Yet You ask me to love my enemies, to bless those who curse me.

◇◇◇

Lord, be more important to me than anyone. May I find my
worth only in You. When You are everything to me, then my
family's actions will no longer matter so much. And when I no
longer need their love and acceptance to know my own
worth, I can finally be free to forgive them.

◇◇◇

Lord, help me to do my best to represent You in my interactions
with my own "crazy uncle." I need Your wisdom to understand
when to step up and say something and when not to, when to show
grace, and when to step back from the relationship. I want to look
past the frustration and disappointment I feel and approach
this relative with kindness and humility (Galatians 6:1).

FAMILY STRESS

O thou afflicted, tossed with tempest, and not comforted, behold, I will set thy stones in fair colors, and lay thy foundations with sapphires.
ISAIAH 54:11 ASV

Family life is full of stress. Relationships, conflicting responsibilities, busy schedules—all of them contribute to the tension that often escalates within our homes. When something out of the ordinary comes along—a death in the family, a fire, a job loss, a serious illness—the stress can mount to nearly unbearable levels.

And yet stress can also be what makes our families strong. When we find ways to meet the challenges together, we draw closer to one another. When we weather another crisis, we can thank God that He has guided our family through the storm. He is building a strong and beautiful foundation for our family's future.

Lord, may even our chores tie us together in a new way. Give us joy and laughter as we wash the dishes or do the laundry, take out the garbage or mop the kitchen floor. May we learn to enjoy our time together.

◇◇◇

With all our busy schedules, God, You know how hard it is to ever find time to sit down together. Help us to make time to share a meal together at least once each day. Draw us together around the table. As we share food, may we also share one another's lives.

◇◇◇

I can't remember the last time we sat down together for a meal. We are coming and going. The work and school schedules are only the beginning. All the extras are what seem to steal our time. Remind us of what's important, God. Help us to prioritize better. We need some downtime, some time to enjoy being a family again. I pray that You'll guide us as we determine what we should cut out in order to lessen our family's stress.

◇◇◇

The stress I'm experiencing is beginning to take over my family life. We used to laugh and play games together. Where did we go wrong? God, I know that I often lash out at my spouse or the kids when they don't deserve it. I let my stress overflow and become my family's stress. Forgive me, Lord, and help me to manage stress better so that it doesn't ruin my family.

You know how stressed our family is, Father. Remind us to set aside time now and then from the rush and hurry, time to simply relax together. Bless us, I pray, and make our family life more fun!

◇◇◇

Help us to slow down, God. The hurry and the busyness of everyday life can be so consuming. Please grant us as parents discernment when we make choices for our family. Family is more important than extracurricular activities or money. Give us wisdom, Father, to know what to say yes to and what things we'd be wise to say no to.

◇◇◇

God, I see my children's stress. I hear it in their bedtime prayers. I miss their easy smiles and silly laughter. We're going through a tough time. Help us to shield our children as much as possible so that adult stress doesn't harm our little ones like this. It breaks my heart, and I know that You don't want them to be so burdened.

◇◇◇

When we're always in such a hurry, God, it's hard to have the energy to address the problems that come up in our family's life. May we never be in too much of a hurry to share our hearts and listen to each other. Help us together to find the solutions to our family's problems.

◇◇◇

Loving Father, You know that sometimes the "adult problems" in our family seem to overshadow the children's. Remind us, Lord, that the death of a goldfish or a cross word from a teacher can be as stressful to our family's younger members as professional challenges and financial worries are to the older ones.

God, I pray that You will guide us as we analyze what's causing the stress we're facing. We know this is not how You want us to live. We must determine what to do about it. Grant us the ability to make changes where changes are possible. Help us to learn to live peacefully and to find creative ways to work around the stresses we cannot eliminate.

◇◇◇

Jesus, help us not to play the blame game but to seek a solution for this stress we're facing. We have to work together on this.

◇◇◇

Family is such a gift. Help us to remember that throughout the year, not just on special occasions like birthdays and Christmas. Help us to be kinder to one another, God. I want our family to be strong. Help me to do what I should do as a leader of this home to help make us a strong family again.

◇◇◇

Jesus, help us not to blame each other for the stress we face. Instead, may we work together and help one another.

◇◇◇

Give us the insight to see which parts of our family's situation can be changed, God. Strengthen us to rise above the circumstances that can't be changed and find ways to live with them creatively.

◇◇◇

Lord, help our family to pray the serenity prayer: "Grant us the serenity to accept the things we cannot change, the courage to change the things we can, and the wisdom to know the difference."

FEAR

*God is our refuge and strength, an ever-present help in trouble.
Therefore we will not fear, though the earth give way
and the mountains fall into the heart of the sea.*

PSALM 46:1–2 NIV

Fear is a normal and healthy biological reaction that alerts us to danger. Unfortunately, in our lives, fear and danger no longer necessarily go together. Instead, fear can exist all on its own. When that happens, fear becomes destructive and crippling. As Franklin D. Roosevelt said, "The only thing we have to fear is fear itself."

When we find ourselves in bondage to fear, God holds the key that can set us free. When life seems threatening, filled with unknown (and possibly imaginary) dangers, He will be our refuge. He is always there. In Him, we can always be secure.

Lord God, You are my shield and my strength. You are my light in the darkness, my shelter in the storm, my strength when I am weak. You shore up my mind against any enemy, whether inside my own head or outside in the world. I am a partaker of Your divine nature and promises (2 Peter 1:4). Your Word tells me not to be anxious (Philippians 4:6), and I am determined to obey You.

◇◇◇

Lord, You are my light and my salvation. Whom shall I fear? You are the strength of my life. Of whom shall I be afraid? When my emotional enemies attack me, they'll stumble and fall. Though an entire army of fears come against me, my heart will be strong. Even in the midst of a war, I can be confident in You, because I ask You for only one thing: that I may dwell in Your house all the days of my life, seeing Your beauty. (Psalm 27:1–4)

◇◇◇

For You, Lord, have not given me a spirit of bondage to fear. Instead, Your Spirit has adopted me. And now, whenever I am scared, I can cry, "Daddy! Father!" (Romans 8:15)

◇◇◇

Lord, sometimes I feel afraid and vulnerable. I fear being alone. I fear failure. I fear opening up, loving and trusting others. I fear things I have no business fearing. You tell me in Your Word that each day has enough trouble of its own and that I need not borrow trouble. Set a guard over my heart, Father, so that I will not fear things I shouldn't. Calm my spirit, I pray, that I might rest in You again.

God, You are my "refuge and strength, an ever-present help in trouble" (Psalm 46:1 NIV). Because of this, I choose not to fear, regardless of what happens.

◇◇◇

Jesus, I will draw You closer than my fears so I can see You instead of them. I will let go of what I cannot control and trust You to protect me and my loved ones. Turn my thoughts to You.

◇◇◇

Thank You, Jesus, that You have given me Your peace. I know Your peace is not like anything the world has to offer me. Because of You, I will not let my heart be troubled, neither will I let it be afraid. (John 14:27)

◇◇◇

Jesus, I've been afraid. I'm tired of fearing silly things—things that are out of my control. You graciously offer me peace—Your peace. It's a peace the world knows nothing of and cannot offer me. If I simply receive Your peace, I know that my heart will not be troubled or afraid (John 14:27).

◇◇◇

Abba Father, when I lay my head on my pillow at night, I will rest in the knowledge that my Creator is in control. I have nothing to fear. You watch over me as I sleep. You have promised never to leave me. You sing over me as I sleep. The powerful, peaceful lullaby of my God.

◇◇◇

You are with me, Lord, so I will not fear. I have You, and because of this, I need not fear what others may do to me. My God is on my side. (Psalm 118:6)

You have given me a spirit of power, of love, and of self-discipline (2 Timothy 1:7). I refuse to fear. I call on the powerful name of God Almighty to see me through. Thank You for fighting for me, Lord.

◇◇◇

God, I want to walk with You, hand in hand, as I face my fears. Show me what it is that really scares me. I will give it to You and trust You to lead, protect, and preserve me every step we take.

◇◇◇

Since You are my light and salvation, Lord, what should I be afraid of? You are my stronghold—so why should I fear anything? (Psalm 27:1)

◇◇◇

You are with me, Lord, so I won't be afraid. What can human beings do to me when I have You? (Psalm 118:6)

◇◇◇

You didn't give me a timid spirit, God, but a spirit of power, of love, and of self-discipline. (2 Timothy 1:7)

◇◇◇

Father, You are the God of second chances. I am embarrassed at how I've let my fear get the best of me. I've let thoughts of what *could* go wrong take me captive instead of taking them captive in obedience to Christ (2 Corinthians 10:3–5). I don't want to miss out on any experience You have for me, including developing a deeper trust in Your protection and provision. Give me another chance to trust You more than my fears.

FINANCIAL STRAIN

My God shall supply every need of yours according to his riches in glory in Christ Jesus.
PHILIPPIANS 4:19 ASV

◆

God uses our financial needs to draw us closer to Him. He hasn't promised that we will be rich, nor does He demand that we be penniless. Instead, He wants us to simply trust Him, whatever our finances. Even in the midst of financial stress, He offers us the prosperity and abundance of His grace. He has promised to meet our every need.

Father, I feel the weight of money problems on my shoulders. You have given me the responsibility of providing for my family, but it seems I can't put a foot right these days. I don't want my heart to tighten up just because my wallet is shrinking. You're bigger than my bank account or my job situation or the unexpected hits our savings have taken lately. Give me Your peace as I set a tone of confidence in Your provision.

◇◇◇

Lord, why am I anxious about having enough money for the clothes I need? Remind me that the flowers of the field don't work or do anything at all, and yet You clothe them gloriously. If You clothe the grass, which is alive for such a fleeting time, remind me that You will certainly clothe me! (Matthew 6:28–30)

◇◇◇

Jesus, money is tight. I seem to run out of it before I run out of days in the month. Please take what I have and stretch it. Give me wisdom in my spending and in places I can cut back. Ultimately, help me to trust You with this money. It's all Yours anyway.

◇◇◇

God, just as You take care of the lilies of the field and the birds of the air, You will take care of me. You know my needs. I don't have to scurry about or worry excessively about money. I simply need to lay this burden down and trust You. You have come through for me before and You will do so this time. I thank You for taking care of me so well. (Matthew 6:28–33)

God, times are pretty lean these days and the bills won't stop coming. But my first debt is to You, for who You are and all You've done for me. I won't stop paying my tithe, even if we get down to the proverbial widow's mite.

◇◇◇

Dear Jesus, help me to continue to give even when there is not as much in my bank account. I know that giving is a blessing to others, but it's also a blessing to the giver. I know that You will provide for me as I continue to follow Your command on my life to give (Luke 6:38).

◇◇◇

God, I have not been wise with my money. You know that I have wasted money on things that did not honor You. Help me to make better choices as I move forward. I want to do better and to honor You with my spending. You are the giver of all good gifts.

◇◇◇

Dear Jesus, help me to follow Your commands. Even when I am financially stressed, may I give to others, knowing that You will give back to me—"good measure, pressed down, shaken together, and running over." You have enough for me—but you will use the same measure to meet my needs that I use to give to others. (Luke 6:38 NKJV)

◇◇◇

Let me not sow sparingly, God. Instead, show me how to scatter seeds everywhere so that I can also reap bountifully. Let me give to others willingly, cheerfully, without grudging. No matter what my finances, I know Your grace will be enough. You will give me all I need to give to others. (2 Corinthians 9:6–8)

God, I give You my finances. I should have done so a long time ago. I thought I had the money under control, but I didn't. It began to get away from me little by little, and here I am in debt that's swallowing up not only me but my family with me. Forgive me and help me, God. I give it all to You, and I ask that You help me to sort it out and to do better with financial responsibility in the future. I want our family to honor You in every area—our finances included.

◇◇◇

Lord, I need to keep the lines of communication with my spouse open about our finances. It's a sore spot and a source of conflict between us. More than ever, we need to be one flesh when it comes to money. We need to be united in searching Your Word for Your will in making decisions, in identifying problems, and in seeking solutions. Don't let money divide us, but let it draw us closer to You and each other in new and powerful ways.

◇◇◇

God, I confess that I am hesitant to share my financial situation with anyone. I think it's because I'm also anxious about being honest with You about it. I know You're fully aware of my attitudes about money, but I ask You to show them to me. Make me aware of what I need to know and what I need to do better. I won't blink. I acknowledge that no amount of money can give me peace if I am not right with You. Forgive me for making money an idol, for letting its importance, even in the form of stress about it, take first place in my heart over You. You are my shelter and my provider. I trust You to take care of me and my family, and I will listen to any wisdom You send me.

Help me to be content with much or with little. My bank account does not define who I am or the degree of happiness in my life. Whether I find myself wealthy or poor, help me to honor You and to be thankful to You for what I have (Philippians 4:11–13, 19).

◇◇◇

Teach me, Jesus, to be content in whatever financial situation I find myself. Teach me how to have next to nothing—and how to have more than enough. In any and every financial circumstance, teach me the secret of facing either plenty or hunger, abundance or need. I believe You will supply my every need from Your riches in glory. (Philippians 4:11–13, 19)

◇◇◇

God, thank You that I can be confident that I can ask You for anything, knowing that You hear me. Since You hear me, You will answer me (1 John 5:14). I give you my finances, Father. I bring all my concerns to You. I trust You to take care of everything.

◇◇◇

Lord God, I've learned some hard lessons about money. One of them is that I am a steward—a caretaker—of what You've given me. You expect me to oversee what You have provided, and if I'm faithful with a little, You're faithful to give me more (Luke 16:10). Starting now, I commit myself to being responsible with my resources—my time, talent, and treasure—and to focusing on what I and my family need, rather than what we want.

FORECLOSURE

*Jesus replied, "Foxes have dens and birds have nests,
but the Son of Man has no place to lay his head."*
LUKE 9:58 NIV

Our homes are important parts of our identity. They give us security and comfort. When we lose them, we feel adrift and frightened. The loss is greater than just a financial problem; it strikes at our very hearts. It doesn't seem possible that we can be forced to give up something so intimately our own. Even birds have nests, and even foxes have holes in the ground they think of as home!

Jesus knew what it was like to be without a home. Once He was an adult, He had no home of His own. He understands how people feel who are forced to give up their houses. He walks with them through this time. And He holds out His arms, longing to offer them the shelter of His love.

God, we are facing foreclosure unless You intervene. It hurts to think that You led us to this home and now we're falling short. Strengthen my faith through this mess. I can't get out of it without You, but I can survive whatever happens with You. I commit my home to You and trust that whatever You allow to happen, You're working it all together for my good.

◇◇◇

Lord, make me a good listener to those who are going through the pain of foreclosure. Let me not judge or be impatient. Give me the wisdom to give good advice. Make me willing to be useful in any way I can be, even if it includes opening my own home.

◇◇◇

God, our economy is so complicated. Remind us that our own mistakes are mixed up with those of many others. We cannot untangle what is already done. Help us to focus instead on the future. May we learn from the past as we move forward. Give us wisdom to plan carefully for whatever comes next.

◇◇◇

Father, I have asked You over and over for help in keeping my house. Now that the foreclosure papers have come, I'm not sure how to feel. I'm disappointed, and the thought of being homeless is more than I can bear. But part of me is relieved to be out from under this debt. Please help me take care of my family as we dig out from under this and find a new place to live.

◇◇◇

I'm so confused, Lord. There are so many legal and financial things to be done. Show me where to seek the knowledge I need to find my way.

Remind us, Father, that our family is more than a house.
Give us places to be together and feel safe. Be with each one
of us, especially the youngest members of our family,
as we struggle to make our way through this difficult time.

◇◇◇

Be our Home now, Creator God. May we realize
in a new way that You are all we truly need to feel safe.

◇◇◇

Lord, I need Your strength and wisdom to lead my family at this
difficult time. You came to give us life—full, overflowing life—
and I don't want that to be tied to a house or a job or a savings
account. You've got a bigger picture in mind than I can see. I
want to lead my family in trusting You, showing Your comfort
and care, and living with the faith that You will take care of us
here—and that we will dwell in Your house forever (Psalm 23:6).

◇◇◇

God, help me to be supportive and comforting to people who
have gone through foreclosure. It's easy to sit off to the side
and make judgments, but let me enter their suffering with
them. Let me be Your hands and feet to show
them that You have not forgotten them.

◇◇◇

I am grieving the loss of our house, Jesus. Remind me
that it's okay to go through all the stages of grief,
and that You will walk with me through each one.

GAMBLING

Keep your lives free from the love of money and be content with what you have, because God has said, "Never will I leave you; never will I forsake you."
HEBREWS 13:5 NIV

With gambling, what starts out as a fun diversion can quickly become a problematic dependency, even for believers. Any time we use something other than prayer and fellowship and seeking God in His Word to relieve stress, anxiety, sorrow, loneliness, or guilt, we're open to sinful addictions.

Many people enjoy the high stakes and excitement of gambling, but some are more susceptible to addiction than others. If you've ever had a problem with drinking or drugs or porn, then gambling is not a safe option for entertainment or stress relief.

Like any addiction, gambling often leads to conflict with spouses and children, problems at work, and issues at church—all of which compound the guilt the gambler already feels, which can drive that person further into isolation and away from help.

Although the Bible doesn't directly forbid gambling, it's a straightforward matter to find principles in scripture that point the Christian away from it. But the same encouragement exists for you as it does for any other addict. With help from a Christian counselor or addiction treatment program—and from God of course—an addict committed to the process of recovery can begin to overcome this dependency and rebuild relationships.

God, somehow I ended up trusting my chances at a casino more than I trusted You. What started as a simple game of chance became an escape from other problems. I felt like a hypocrite for even thinking about looking in Your Word or praying. But I see now that separation from You was not what You wanted but what Satan wanted for me. Deliver me from his lies (and my own).

◇◇◇

Lord, I am tired of all the lies I've told myself and others to cover my problem—and of all the justification and rationalization I've used to defend what I called recreation. You are the God of truth, not lies (Isaiah 65:16; Hebrews 6:18), so help me to embrace Your truth.

◇◇◇

Lord God, my gambling is a serious problem. I have gambled without any thought or concern for Your glory, for taking care of my family, for loving my neighbors, or for working for what I need—all things the Bible says we should do. Forgive me, Lord, for trusting odds more than You.

◇◇◇

Father, I'm supposed to live my life depending on You for all I need (Matthew 6:33, Philippians 4:19). I haven't been, though. Instead, my gambling has caused financial hardship for me and my family, with whom I have also broken trust by spending money in casinos that I should have used to care for them. I've ruined my good reputation, and I'm on the verge of despair. I need to stop. Help me *want* to stop. Give me the guts to confess my sin to my spouse and family, to get help, and to find accountability. Help me face the repercussions of my actions and learn what I need to do to follow You and earn back the trust of those I've hurt.

GOING THROUGH CHANGE

*"For I have come down from heaven not to do my
will but to do the will of him who sent me."*
JOHN 6:38 NIV

Change is a natural part of life. Very little stays the same. Whether you're experiencing a change associated with joy or sorrow, you will need to rely on God to help you adjust.

For many of us, we crave routine and sameness. It makes us feel secure. A sense of stability is very important. When something changes in our lives, it may leave us feeling unsettled or afraid. Remember that Jesus experienced change. He left heaven to come down to earth and be born as a baby—not in a royal palace but in a stable for animals. Talk about change! He understands the jolt that a sudden shift in one's reality can bring.

Pray that the Holy Spirit will enable you to embrace rather than resist change. Change can be a glorious thing, opening new avenues and bringing new adventures that you might have otherwise missed.

God, I don't like change. I'll admit it. I like the comforting
feeling of knowing what each day will bring. Not having this
has brought some anxiety into my life. Please help
me look to You to help me adjust.

◇◇◇

Father, this change has caught me unaware. I wasn't ready for
it or expecting it. I didn't have time to prepare. Please come
alongside me and show me the way I should react to it.
Give me grace to accept it and to find the positives
even though it's an unwanted change in my life.

◇◇◇

God, I know that not all change is bad. It can be invigorating!
Today I pray for a new perspective. Help me to embrace the
changes that have come my way. Help me to enjoy them even.

◇◇◇

Some people seem to thrive on change. They move frequently
and take new jobs. They enjoy variety. I wish I were more like
that. I like routines and regularity. This change has shaken up
my nice, predictable world. I find myself in a panic. Calm my
spirit, Father. Remind me that You have not left me.
We will walk through this time of adjustment
together. Thank You for being near.

There is a time for everything and a purpose for everything that happens (Ecclesiastes 3:1). I know this change is not a surprise to You, Lord. You see all the pieces of the puzzle that make up my life. I can only see one piece at a time. You see how this "new normal" is going to draw me closer to You and how it will challenge and shape me. Please allow this change in my life to bring You glory, just as everything should. I love You, Lord.

◇◇◇

You know the plans You have for me, Sovereign God. Your plans are never to hurt me but always to bring me hope. You have a good future in store for me (Jeremiah 29:11). Help me to look at this change as just a part of the plan. Thank You for assuring me that You are still in control even when things seem a bit out of control in my little world.

◇◇◇

God, I know there is one thing that will never change. You will never leave me. Even if my job changes. . .even if I must move across the country. . .even if I'm abandoned by others. . . even if I grow ill or disabled and cannot live the way I'm used to. . .You will be there. You will never leave me or forsake me (Deuteronomy 31:8). I take great comfort in Your faithfulness and loyalty, heavenly Father.

GREED

Then he said, "Beware! Guard against every kind of greed.
Life is not measured by how much you own."
LUKE 12:15 NLT

◆

We've often heard it said that money is the root of all evil. Actually, however, the Bible says that *the love of* money is the root of evil (1 Timothy 6:10). In other words, it's greed that gets us in trouble. Money itself is merely a useful tool, which can be used for either good or bad.

But greed is the urge to get more and more of something, whether it be money or food or possessions. The greedy person is too attached to the things of this world. And as a result, the greedy person is often anxious, worried about losing what they already have.

The generous person, however, is truly free. They can open their hands and take the good things God brings into their life. And they can just as easily let these things go. It gives them joy to share, and loss doesn't cause them worry. The generous person knows that God has plenty to give, and His grace will never be exhausted.

Father, forgive me for the way I have rationalized my focus on getting more and more things. I've put "keeping up with the Joneses" ahead of keeping my eyes on You—and I've tried to justify my acquisitions as by-products of Your blessings. Show me the real problem behind my behavior, no matter how hard it is for me to learn. My desire for things has alienated me from You, and it has kept me from being the person You made me to be: a source of blessing, not merely a receptacle.

◇◇◇

Lord, my greed has disguised itself as good, but everything I get leaves me feeling unsatisfied—and I realize that's not Your best for me. I've found myself thinking, *I deserve that* or *If I don't get this, I'll be missing out.* Forgive me for thinking of You as my genie instead of my God. I want to honor You by representing You well in every part of my life, especially my finances.

◇◇◇

Dearest Lord, remind me that when I am greedy and acquisitive, someone else often pays the price. My abundance may deprive others of what they truly need. Make me willing to get by with less so that others will have enough. Teach me to share.

◇◇◇

Jesus, reveal to me my greed. Help me to recognize my true priorities. Make me see where I spend too much. Show me things I could do without. Help me resist the persistent voices that come at me constantly in commercials and ads, telling me I need more. Create in me a generous heart.

◇◇◇

What good are riches, Lord, if I don't use them to help others?

Jesus, you made it clear that You expect a return on Your investment in us (Luke 19:11–27)—which shows that money can be used to make a profit without greed. I want to use what You give me to bless my family and my community, to bring people into Your kingdom, and to make my finances part of my witness for Your glory.

◇◇◇

Show me, God, that greed weighs me down. When greed rules my heart, I am never satisfied. I can't enjoy what I have, because I'm too focused on what I don't have.

◇◇◇

Give me pleasure, heavenly Father, in the things that are truly most important, the things that cannot be accumulated. . . like a child's laugh, a friend's presence, or a beautiful sunset.

◇◇◇

God, I repent of not being content with what You have given me. I've gotten what I want mixed up with what I need, and that's because I've taken my eyes off You and set them on what I think You should provide. I've made an idol of money, putting it in a higher place in my heart than You. Forgive me, and teach me to be content, to give, and to trust Your provision.

◇◇◇

Remind me, Lord, that my value does not depend on what I own. Instead, may I see that greed comes between You and me, between others and me, and even between me and my true self.

◇◇◇

Help me, Christ Jesus, to put to death within me all that leads me away from You. Destroy my greed, for when I am greedy, I am worshipping false gods. Let me only worship You. (Colossians 3:5)

GRIEF

"Blessed are those who mourn, for they will be comforted."
MATTHEW 5:4 NIV

Grief follows when we lose someone to death, but we also grieve for the living. We can even grieve dreams that didn't turn out as we had imagined. Perhaps you were abandoned by a parent or by your spouse. In many ways, the one who left you is dead to you now. You must walk through grief. If you've experienced abuse, you must grieve your innocence or the trust that once came so easily. You may have had your childhood stolen from you at a young age due to sexual abuse. Grief is the result.

Recognizing that grief comes as a result of loss is very important. Whether you've lost a dear relative or friend to death or experienced another type of loss, grief is natural. You'll be in shock or denial. You'll feel anger and sadness. You may try to bargain with God. You'll pass through the stages of grief. But one day you will recover. The loss will still be there, but the pain will lessen. Trust God to walk with you. Ask Him to hold you close as you grieve. Cry out to Him. He is there.

Dearest Lord, I'm grieving a loss that was long ago. It comes back to me at certain seasons of the year. A situation or a phrase can catch me so unaware. I find myself transported back to another time and another place. The loss feels just as deep and the grief just as strong as it was back then. Comfort me with Your Holy Spirit, I pray. This is a deep loss, and I must not try to brush it off as less. I must acknowledge the pain so that You can provide a healing balm to my soul.

◇◇◇

I need You, God. I can't walk through this alone. I'm grieving for one who still lives. It's harder, I think, than grieving for the dead. This person is not part of my life anymore, but this is not my choice. I simply must accept the decision another has made and walk through the grief that is the result. I can't control all of the losses in my life. Walk with me, God. We can do this together. I can do it if You stay with me and assure me that You will never leave.

◇◇◇

Jesus, I'm filled with grief. I feel like I cannot go on. I've lost a part of me. I don't feel like me anymore. Hold me close. I know that grief is the price we pay for love. I pay it gladly. I would love again just as fully even knowing that this is how it would feel in the end.

◇◇◇

I have loved and I have lost. It's part of the human existence. The beauty of grieving for a believer in Christ is that we don't have to grieve as the world does. We grieve as those who have hope! We will see our loved one again. We will be together in heaven for all eternity. This is just a "see ya" rather than a final goodbye.

I'm waiting for You, Lord. I know You will lean down to me and hear my cry. You will draw me up out of the pit of destruction, this miry bog of grief and sadness where I'm stuck. You will set my feet on the rock, and You will make my steps steady. And then You will put a new song in my mouth, a song of praise to God. Many will see what You have done for me, and they too will put their trust in You. (Psalm 40:1–3)

◇◇◇

Dear God, I feel as though I'm in a desert place, a barren and howling wasteland, where I'm lost, alone, heartbroken. Shield me, Lord. Care for me. Guard me as the apple of Your eye. (Deuteronomy 32:10)

◇◇◇

Heavenly Father, why is my soul so cast down? Why do I feel such turmoil? Help me to hope in You. I know I will again praise You, for You are my salvation and my God. (Psalm 42:11)

◇◇◇

I praise You, the Father of compassion and the God of all comfort, who comforts me now so that I will be able to comfort those around me with the same comfort I receive from God. (2 Corinthians 1:3–4)

◇◇◇

My flesh and my heart may fail, Lord, but You are the strength of my heart and my portion forever (Psalm 73:26).

◇◇◇

My comfort in this, God, is that Your promises save me (Psalm 119:50). Help me to trust in them.

Lord, You reached down from above. You took and drew me
up out of grief's deep waters. You delivered me from my strong
enemy, from this sorrow that was too strong for me to overcome
on my own. When life threatened to knock me off my feet,
You held me steady. You brought me forth into a large place,
a place of freedom and emotional health. You delivered me
because I delighted You. (2 Samuel 22:17–20)

◇◇◇

I am in distress; my eyes are sore with grief; my soul and my
body are exhausted. My strength is gone, and my body
has let me down. Be gracious to me, O Lord.
Come and help me! (Psalm 31:9–10).

◇◇◇

Grief is like a roller coaster, Father, and I'm so tired of riding.
I want to forget. I want to get off this tumultuous, up-and-down
cycle. And yet, I know that shutting down my emotions is
not healthy. I must ride this out. Will You come with me?
Will You sit beside me so I can cling to You when I'm afraid?
I need You, Father, as I ride out this deep period of grief.

◇◇◇

I'm grieving the loss of a friendship, Lord. I remember when
this friendship was light and fun, a positive thing in my life.
But that was a long, long time ago. You have clearly shown me
it was time to walk away. I know that ending this relationship
was best for me. But it doesn't take away the sadness
I feel. It's hard to let go of someone I love.

GUILT

Blessed is the one whose transgressions are forgiven, whose sins are covered.
PSALM 32:1 NIV

The Lord forgives. He is your hiding place. He will not let the waters reach you and overtake you. He keeps His loving eyes on you and guides you and instructs you. He protects you from trouble and surrounds you with songs of deliverance.

These are all promises found in Psalm 32. To claim this freedom and victory in Jesus, your part is simply to confess. Sounds easy enough. . .but sometimes we carry unnecessary guilt for far too long when we've done something wrong.

Learn to go to God quickly. Be honest with Him. He has seen your sin. He knows you through and through. There is no hiding iniquity from God. Sometimes confession of guilt is a very difficult and emotional thing. We must not avoid it though. Just as we plunged into the waywardness that led us here, we must plunge into the forgiving arms of our Lord. What comfort there is to be found in the arms of Jesus!

Remind me today, God, that I can't change the past. I feel guilty for the things I've done and the people I've hurt. Transform these feelings of guilt into encouragement to move forward as a changed person. Wallowing in my guilt will not do any good, but praying for the strength to do better in the future will.

◇◇◇

I confess my sin to You in these moments, loving Lord. I fall before You, weary from the burden I've been carrying. I release it all to You. I am so sorry for my sin. It hurts my heart to know that my sin hurt You and displeased You. Lift this load of guilt, my Savior. Forgive me, I pray.

◇◇◇

Lord, sometimes when I feel guilty, it comes out in other forms. I grow angry. I'm short with those I love. I avoid people or places that remind me of my sin. All of these things impact others around me. They're not healthy for my marriage, and they don't strengthen my bond with my children or grandchildren. My coworkers suffer as well. Father, please forgive me and help me to walk as a forgiven child of the King as I move forward.

◇◇◇

Thank You, Lord, for not counting my sin against me. Thank You for washing me white as snow through the blood of Jesus. I don't have to hang my head in shame or guilt. Jesus died once and for all. A supernatural stain lifter, He removed my guilt. Hallelujah! I am free.

Jesus, You paid a debt I could not pay. I was guilty of sin.
You were a spotless Lamb, without blemish. You took upon
your shoulders the sin of the whole world. You died a terrible
death as the innocent Son of God to make a way for guilty
sinners like me to come into the presence of a holy God.
I am forever grateful to You for paying my debt.

◇◇◇

I know, Father, that I cannot keep Your laws perfectly. If I break
even one law, I've broken them all (James 2:10). That's why I
need a Savior. That's why I need Jesus. Forgive me, I pray,
and wake me up tomorrow ready to face a new day in a new way.

◇◇◇

Thank You, God, that when You look at me,
You see me through a Jesus lens. Perfect and blameless,
clothed in righteousness, forgiven and free.

HELPLESSNESS

"But the tax collector stood at a distance. He would not even look up to heaven, but beat his breast and said, 'God, have mercy on me, a sinner.'"
LUKE 18:13 NIV

We've all heard the expression, "God helps those who help themselves." And while there's a certain truth to the saying (God doesn't want to sit there expecting a miracle when He's already put the means to accomplish something into our hands), the opposite is also true: God helps those who are helpless.

Look at the tax collector who didn't even try to prove his worth. He just stood off at a distance and threw himself on God's mercy. Alcoholics Anonymous teaches that only when people have hit rock bottom and finally acknowledge their helplessness are they ready to change.

In Jesus' day, the Pharisees didn't see themselves as helpless. They trusted in their own righteousness, in their own abilities to save themselves. But Jesus said, "Blessed are the poor in spirit, for theirs is the kingdom of heaven" (Matthew 5:3 NIV). When we are helpless, when we give up our dependence on our own strength, then God can begin to act in our lives.

I need You, God. I can't handle life on my own.

◇◇◇

Lord, You promise to give me all that I need.
I depend on You for my help.

◇◇◇

God, I see that the times I feel helpless are the times I haven't understood or acted in the power and authority You have given me as Your child. I may not know the answers to the problems around me, but You do. If I act on my own, my helplessness will increase. But if I act as Your servant and in alignment with Your will (which I know from reading Your Word), You will give me the power I need to do what You want me to do. Your "divine power has given to [me] all things that pertain to life and godliness" (2 Peter 1:3 NKJV).

◇◇◇

Lord, help me to know the difference between accepting that I need Your help—and using a false helplessness to manipulate others. Show me all You have already given me, and give me the insight to use it.

◇◇◇

I need You, God. I can't handle life on my own.

◇◇◇

Lord, You promise to give me all that I need.
I depend on You for my help.

◇◇◇

Jesus, I can't control my life anymore. I don't know where to turn. I give up. Please, take over.

I know You have the strength I need, heavenly Father.
Give me a new perspective, I pray. Instead of worrying about
my own weakness, help me to glory in Your power.

◇◇◇

Since I am surrounded by such a huge crowd of witnesses to the
life of faith, help me, dear Jesus, to strip off every weight that
slows me down, especially the sin that so easily trips me up.
Help me to run with endurance the race You have set before me.
I know that keeping my eyes on You, the champion who initiates
and perfects my faith, is the only way I'll have strength to do
this. Because of the joy awaiting You, You endured the cross,
disregarding its shame—so if You did that, when I feel like giving
up remind me of all You endured for me. (Hebrews 12:1–3)

◇◇◇

Lord, You know the hopes of the helpless. Surely You will
hear my cries and comfort me (Psalm 10:17).

◇◇◇

Thank You, God, for pouring out Your love into my
heart through the Holy Spirit, whom You have given to me.
For at just the right time, when I was completely helpless,
Christ came and gave Himself for me. (Romans 5:5–6)

◇◇◇

Sometimes, Lord Jesus, when I feel helpless, I'm really just
underestimating the abilities You've given me. Give me the
strength and confidence to become the person
You created me to be.

Lord, I want to understand the greatness of Your power, which gives me the wisdom and ability I need to accomplish Your will in my life and in the world around me. Your Spirit in me clothes me with Your power to go out and represent You. I ask You for the wisdom to understand and access "the exceeding greatness of [Your] power toward us who believe" (Ephesians 1:19 NKJV), the same power that raised Christ from the dead and set Him above all things. That's the power in me to be the person You've called me to be.

◇◇◇

Jesus, release me from these feelings of helplessness. I want to be who You've called me to be, and I want to live under Your authority just as You lived under the Father's while You were on earth. Forgive me for any lack of obedience, for any desire to choose my way over Yours, so that I can fulfill Your promise that "anyone who believes in me will do the same works I have done, and even greater works" (John 14:12 NLT).

◇◇◇

Sometimes, Father, I feel helpless to change the way others perceive me. Thank You that You always believe in me.

God, I'm done with this learned helplessness in my life. My unbelief has compromised Your authority and power in my life. There have been times when I didn't see You working in my life or in the world around me, and I assumed that, because I couldn't see it, You wouldn't work or You didn't care. Help my unbelief (Mark 9:24), cast out my fear with Your perfect love (1 John 4:18), and cleanse me of rebellious thoughts (Psalm 51:10). Jesus said, "As the Father has sent me, even so I am sending you" (John 20:21 ESV). Here I am.

◇◇◇

God, give me a healthy humility that depends on Your strength as my help and refuge. May my sense of helplessness not be based on lies I tell myself, however. When I hear myself saying things like, "There's no way I can get out of this mess—it's hopeless," or "Life hasn't been fair to me, so why should I even try anymore?" or "No one cares about me so I might as well give up," remind me that these words are not the truth. Give me the courage that's based on confidence in Your strength.

◇◇◇

Father, Your Word says, "The helpless commits himself to You; You are the helper of the fatherless" (Psalm 10:14 NKJV). I feel like there's no way out of the situation I'm in, but I know that nothing is impossible for You. As the psalmist prayed, "My help comes from the LORD, the Maker of heaven and earth" (Psalm 121:2 NIV). I am not trapped, and I am not helpless because I am Yours.

HIDDEN SIN

"People look at the outward appearance, but the Lord looks at the heart."
1 Samuel 16:7 niv

If sin is anything that comes between God and us, then we are simply deceiving ourselves if we think there's any point in burying our sins out of sight where no one can see it. Sin that is hidden still gets in the way of our relationship with God. By hiding it out of sight, we may think we have fooled other people. We may even fool ourselves. We do not fool God.

In the New Testament, Paul makes it clear that our hidden thoughts are just as serious and damaging as our external behaviors. He wants us to be people of integrity and wholeness, without any darkness festering inside us. He knows that ultimately, it is our own selves that are hurt most by these shameful secrets.

Lord, "When I kept silent, my bones wasted away through my
groaning all day long. . . . Then I acknowledged my sin to
you and did not cover up my iniquity" (Psalm 32:3, 5 NIV).
David's confession convicts me. Thank You for
forgiving me. Teach me Your ways.

◇◇◇

In the Gospels, You said that everything that is covered up
will be revealed, and everything that's hidden will be known.
The things I thought I said when I was all alone will be
proclaimed from the housetops (Luke 12:2–3).
How embarrassing! Give me the courage, Lord,
to bring my sin into the light of Your Spirit.

◇◇◇

God, this hidden sin eats away at my heart. I have no peace
because of it. Help me to run from it so that it will not have
power over me any longer. The temptation is great,
but I don't want to return to it anymore.

◇◇◇

Father, there are no secrets with You. You knit me together in
my mother's womb. There I was still just a secret, and You knew
me even then! What makes me think I can hide sin from You?
I choose today to bring this hidden sin into the light. Forgive
me, Lord, for hiding from You as Adam and Eve did in
the garden. I want to be right with You again.

◇◇◇

There are habits that I've developed that don't line up with who
I say I am. I go to church on Sunday and worship You through
song, but my worship stops at the door. I'm leading a double
life, and I want to come clean before You, Father, and before
my family. I am so tired. Please give me the courage to confess.

Examine my heart. If You find any wicked way there, bring it into the light. I don't want anything to come between You and me, Father.

◇◇◇

God, this hidden sin eats away at my heart. I have no peace because of it. Help me to give it to You.

◇◇◇

God, I want to see my sin the way You do—as something that keeps me from a closer relationship with You. When I think about it like that, it seems silly to try to hide anything from You. Show me anything that might create distance between us.

◇◇◇

Keeping up the act is a drain on me. I act one way but I'm covering up what lies beneath the surface. My thought life is not what it should be, and lately some of my actions have frightened me. I feel like I'm just one step away from blatant rebellion. Draw me back to You, Father, before it's too late.

◇◇◇

Nothing is covered up or hidden.
In the end, all will be known (Luke 12:2).

◇◇◇

I come before You with dirty hands and a dirty heart. I know that the wages of sin is death. I feel as if I'm a dead person somehow still walking around among the living. I confess this sin to You, Father. I ask You to forgive me in the powerful name of Jesus and set me on a new course for my life.

◇◇◇

God, I gaze into the mirror of Your Word.
Reveal to me anything that comes between us.

Jesus, show me the sins I hide even from myself. Reveal to me the unhealthy thought habits I cling to. Remind me that if I nurse my hatred toward another, then I am guilty of spiritual murder. And if I allow lustful thoughts to become an obsession, then I am committing the essence of adultery.

◇◇◇

Teach me, Lord, to never be dishonest with myself or You. Examine my heart, and reveal its contents. May there be no secrets between us.

◇◇◇

God, be merciful to me. I look inside myself and see so many shadows. I'm grateful that they stand out in contrast to the light of Your Spirit in me, convicting me of my sin. Cleanse me and fill me with Your Spirit, so that I won't keep sinning against You.

◇◇◇

I realize, Lord, that when I act as though I'm a good and righteous person, all the while hiding my sins out of sight, then I'm also guilty of hypocrisy. Hypocrisy lies around my heart like a wall, keeping others out, keeping You out.

◇◇◇

Jesus, You called hypocrisy the "leaven of the Pharisees" (Luke 12:1). It's something that ferments inside me. It grows, doubles, fills me up—the way yeast does. Remove it from me, I pray. Clean out my heart.

◇◇◇

Father, my sin has found me out (Numbers 32:23), as it always does. Thank You for Your promise: "If we confess our sins, he is faithful and just to forgive us our sins and to cleanse us from all unrighteousness" (1 John 1:9 ESV).

HOPELESSNESS

"For I know the plans I have for you," declares the LORD, "plans to prosper you and not to harm you, plans to give you hope and a future."
JEREMIAH 29:11 NIV

We tend to think of hope as a cheery, optimistic outlook on life. But the biblical concept of hope is far greater and deeper. It is a confidence and expectation in what God will do in the future, an understanding that the same God who was with us yesterday will be with us tomorrow.

When things seem hopeless, we are robbed of this confidence. We feel as though the future is empty and barren. But hopelessness is always a lie, for our God has big plans for us! No matter how hard the road, it always leads us into His presence.

Jesus, nothing in the Bible tells me to ask only when I feel hopeful or strong or capable; there's only the instruction to ask. Ask, You said, and it will be given (Matthew 7:7). You didn't say what would be given, or how, or when—all the things I feel would give me hope. But You told me to ask, and that means You care about what I want and need. The rest I leave to You: "And now, O Lord, for what do I wait? My hope is in you" (Psalm 39:7 ESV).

◇◇◇

Why do I get so depressed, Lord? Why do I surrender my peace? Help me to hope in You, knowing that soon I will be praising You for all You have done. You are the one who will make me smile again. You are my God. (Psalm 43:5)

◇◇◇

Lord, I put my hope in You, for Your love never fails (Psalm 130:7).

◇◇◇

Father, You love me with an everlasting love (Jeremiah 31:3). Your love is my hope and peace and joy.

◇◇◇

Thank You, God, that You have plans for me—plans to bless me and prosper me. I know that Your plans are often not the same as mine. But You know what the future holds, and I trust You.

◇◇◇

Jesus, You promised to never leave me or forsake me. Because of You, I have hope. I know this hope will never be put to shame.

God, I've run into so many dead ends lately. I've made some
bad decisions, and others have made decisions that affected me
negatively. My trust has been betrayed, so I feel like I'm going
out on a limb to say this: I trust that what is impossible
with me is possible with You (Luke 18:27).

◇◇◇

When I feel hopeless, Jesus, remind me that You love me just
as much as Your Father loves You. You—the Son of God,
the Word that existed from before the beginning of the
world—love me, infinitely, unconditionally,
with all Your heart! May I take hope in Your love.

◇◇◇

Remind me, loving Lord, that the world I see with my physical
eyes is only a piece of reality, a glimpse into an enormous
and mysterious universe. Even if I can't see what's going on,
You are doing amazing, mysterious, beautiful things!

◇◇◇

When I can't sense Your presence with me, God, give me grace
to believe that I will one day soon experience Your joy again.

◇◇◇

Praise be to You, the God and Father of my Lord Jesus Christ!
In Your great mercy You have given me new birth into a living
hope through the resurrection of Jesus Christ from the dead.
Through Jesus, I have an inheritance that can never perish,
spoil, or fade. This inheritance is kept in heaven for me,
and in the meantime, through faith I am shielded by God's
power until the coming of the salvation You will eventually
reveal to me. Remind me that even though I have to suffer
grief and trials for a little while now, I can still
rejoice in You, my God of living hope. (1 Peter 1:3–6)

I'm groaning in my heart, Lord, moaning and crying out for You. My body needs Your salvation. This is the hope that saves me. And I know that if I didn't have to wait for Your healing, I wouldn't need to hope. Who hopes for what they already have? So I hope for what I do not yet have, waiting, trying to be patient, while Your Spirit helps my weakness. I don't even know how to pray; I don't know what I should ask You to do—but Your Spirit intercedes for me. And I know that in all things You work for my good, working to shape me into the image of Your Son. (Romans 8:24–29)

◇◇◇

Lord, I'm having a hard time seeing any of the great plans Your Word says You have for me. My life has not gone the way I had hoped and prayed it would, and I can feel the anger and frustration giving way to despair. As David prayed, "You know how I am scorned, disgraced and shamed; all my enemies are before you. . . . I looked for sympathy, but there was none, for comforters, but I found none" (Psalm 69:19–20 NIV). Don't hide from me, Lord! I need You.

◇◇◇

I called to You, Lord, out of my distress—and You answered me! When I was drowning, surrounded by an ocean of despair, with waves billowing over my head, I was sure that You were no longer paying attention to my life. I felt as though I was about to be destroyed. I was sure my life was over. But You brought me up from the pit of despair, Lord. You heard my prayer, even when I felt as though I was spiritually fainting. Lord, help me not to put my trust in anything or anyone but You. When I do, I forsake it to put my hope in Your steadfast love. My salvation comes from You! (Jonah 2:2–7)

INFERTILITY

Hannah was in deep anguish, crying bitterly as she prayed to the Lord. And she made this vow: "O Lord of Heaven's Armies, if you will look upon my sorrow and answer my prayer and give me a son, then I will give him back to you."
1 Samuel 1:10–11 NLT

When you can't become pregnant, it suddenly seems as though every woman you see is expecting. Everywhere you turn, there are reminders that you cannot achieve this thing you long for. From diaper commercials to the unthinking questions of people wondering when you're going to start your family, you feel bombarded by your lack. You may feel as though you are unworthy, worthless. Even in this day of women's rights, you may still believe that your value, your personhood, your fulfillment all depend on your ability to have a child.

God wants you to see this as a lie. The longing for a child is a perfectly natural one. But when we become obsessed with wanting anything—no matter how good it might be—we turn it into a god. Our value does not depend on our ability to do anything. It comes from God—and we can trust Him to fulfill the deepest longings of our hearts in the way that is best for us.

Lord God, I think of biblical examples of people who brought
their infertility before You and You gave them a child:
Isaac and Rebekah (Genesis 25:21), Jacob and Rachel
(Genesis 30:22–24), and Elkanah and Hannah (1 Samuel 1:27),
to name a few. Add our names to that list, Lord.

◇◇◇

Lord, I'm trying to accept whatever You want for my life.
But it's so hard. You know how much I long for a
child. Help me to give this longing to You.

◇◇◇

Lord, help me to give this desire to You. Help me to surrender
it. I have laid down other dreams over the years. This one is
perhaps my deepest desire. I really want a child. Help me to
trust You more as I wait and as I live with this longing.

◇◇◇

God, I know You are a God who works miracles. You are able
to do the impossible. I ask You to allow me to become
pregnant if it is Your will that I bear a child.

◇◇◇

Be with my husband. He wants a child too, but we are so
different as we react to infertility. Please help this draw
us closer together rather than drive us apart.

God, I know You can work miracles. Work in me.
Work in my body. I surrender myself to You.

◇◇◇

I remember playing dolls as a little girl, God. I never dreamed
I wouldn't have a house full of children when I grew up.
Now I would give anything just for one child! Please fulfill
this desire of my heart if it's Your will for me.

◇◇◇

It seems so easy for other women to become pregnant. Not me.
Why must I be the odd one out? Why is it impossible for me to
have a baby? Calm my heart, God. I'm so upset, and I know that
this is not Your desire for me. You want me to trust You more.

◇◇◇

Help my husband as well, Lord. May our longing for a child
not drive us apart. Give us patience with each other's different
perspectives. Whether or not we ever have a child,
may our marriage always be fruitful.

God, they are everywhere—pregnant women and women with
newborn babies. Please help me to rejoice with others and to
celebrate new life. I don't want to be a jealous person.
My heart longs for motherhood, but even in this
difficult place I pray that I can be happy for others.

◇◇◇

I know that You can allow me to get pregnant, but I guess I
wonder if You will. So far, each month I get my hopes up,
and each month my hopes are dashed. You are the giver of life,
and I know that if or when You desire for me to have a baby,
You will bring about a pregnancy. Help me to believe that
You will do whatever is right and best for our family.

◇◇◇

Father, I want to carry my wife's burden in this hard time.
I can't do anything about whether we have a child; that's up
to You. Strengthen me when I'm exhausted and discouraged,
and empower me to love her and show her grace. And by
Your Spirit, lessen those burdens on her heart.

Heavenly Father, I surrender this longing. I lay down the desire.
I'm weary from this burden. I'm tired. I can bear this alone no
longer. I need You to help me. I need You to calm my spirit
and dry my tears. I am sad and frustrated, but even still,
I will praise You, my Creator and Sustainer.

◇◇◇

God, I am hurt and angry at my inability to help create a baby.
My manhood has never felt so assaulted. I need Your help to
deal with these feelings in a healthy way. The last thing I want to
do is hurt my wife further by taking out my frustrations on her.
It's just hard to talk about, so I'm bringing my pain to You.

◇◇◇

I'm seeking You, Lord. You promised that You would answer
me and deliver me from all my fears. You know how much I fear
that I will never be a mother, and so, in the face of my fear,
I claim that promise as my own. I praise You that You are with
me, that I have no need to feel discouraged or worried about
any fertility issues that may lie ahead. Thank you that You are my
strength and my help. Bring peace to my troubled heart as
You uphold me with Your righteous right hand.
(Psalm 34:4; Isaiah 41:10; John 14:27)

I feel so angry and frustrated that I can't become pregnant, God.
Please calm my heart with Your love, for Your love is patient
and kind, and not easily angered. Help me to be slow in my
speech and slow in anger when it comes to dealing with
my spouse, my family members, friends, or my doctor.
Transform my anger into something creative, Lord,
something that can be used for Your glory.

◇◇◇

There are so many dreams tied up in trying to obey You by being
fruitful and multiplying—names we picked, characteristics we
hoped they'd inherit (and others they wouldn't), things they'd
accomplish, and adventures we'd have together. It hurts so much
that it's hard to even think about it. Comfort us in our sorrow.

◇◇◇

God, I am struggling with envy and jealousy as I see pregnant
women and hear of new babies in others' lives. Teach me not to
compare my life with others. Free me from the bitterness
that lives inside me, so that I can rejoice in
the new life You send into the world.

Each month, Lord, I am filled with hope again—and then
each month, my hopes are dashed again. I am tired of
hoping. I don't know how to keep going. Lead me,
loving Lord. Make the way ahead clear to me.

◇◇◇

Heavenly Father, You put into my heart this desire to be a
mother. You have promised to give me the desires of my heart—
and so I trust this desire to You. I believe that even if You don't
satisfy my desires in the way I hope, You will never forget
or overlook any heart's desire. I will delight myself
in You, trusting in Your love. (Psalm 37:4)

◇◇◇

Father, You know we'd love to have a child. I am fighting feelings
of incompleteness and inability at the thought of our infertility.
You are in control, though, and I trust You. I am trying to bear
in mind that I am complete in Christ—that when I face
a test of faith like this, it produces perseverance,
and perseverance produces maturity (James 1:2–4).

INJUSTICE

Do what is fair and just to your neighbor.
MICAH 6:8 MSG

Did you know that in the Gospels, Jesus talks more about justice for those who are poor than He does about violence or sexual immorality? In fact, about a tenth of all the verses in the four Gospels have to do with concern for the poor.

We live in a world of injustice. A third of all the children in the world's developing nations suffer from malnutrition. Almost 3 million children die each year from hunger. This isn't fair. And God cares.

He wants us to care too. He doesn't want us to look away from the world's injustice. He wants us to face it—and fight it.

Jesus, I want to value each person the way You do—especially those society tends to ignore, but also those society tends to hate. Even though Your image has become obscured in all of us, I want to look for it in everyone I meet. I may not be able to see it, but only You can know people's hearts with certainty. It's my job to humble myself, learn about others' needs, and ask to see them through Your eyes. Let me help where I can.

◇◇◇

Lord, You say to me, "Do justice and righteousness, and deliver from the hand of the oppressor those who have been robbed of their rights. Do no harm to those who are aliens and strangers. Don't hurt the children and women who live in single-parent families" (Jeremiah 22:3). Give me the courage and the faith to fight injustice wherever I see it.

◇◇◇

Father, my heart hurts when I look at all the pain and suffering in the world. I want to help, to make some kind of difference for Your glory and for the increase of Your kingdom, but I don't know where to start. Help me see what's getting in my way—being too busy, fear of the messiness of other people's lives, lack of skills, whatever it may be—and then help me keep my eyes on You as You call me to get involved.

◇◇◇

God, you call me to share what I have with those who have less than me (Proverbs 22:16). You ask me to be kind to strangers, to those who are aliens in our land (Exodus 22:21). You remind me to treat with respect those who have apparently lower positions than I do (Job 31:13–14).

God, forgive me for my self-righteousness. I have looked at all the trouble in the world and said, like a certain Pharisee, "Thank You that I'm not as bad as that guy" (Luke 18:10–14). But while I may not be as badly behaved as some, without the blood of Christ, I am just as bad off as anyone. We've all fallen short of Your standard; we all need a Savior. I need You, God. As Your child, I want to get involved in the family business—the good and just work You are doing to restore life and renew hope in individual hearts and across the world. Help me to look past all the injustice and offer hope for a just day to come.

◇◇◇

Lord, when the world treats me unfairly,
remind me of what You endured.

◇◇◇

Give me Your attitude, Jesus. May I think less about what I deserve, and more about the other person. Show me how to turn the other cheek when I am injured (Matthew 5:39). Help me to always follow Your example. Remind me that vengeance is never justice.

◇◇◇

Lord, as I look at a world that both fascinates and infuriates me, I'm torn about how to respond. But then I remember that You called me to fight injustice with mercy and righteousness: "Religion that is pure and undefiled before God the Father is this: to visit orphans and widows in their affliction, and to keep oneself unstained from the world" (James 1:27 ESV). Keep the world and all its sin from staining me with hatred and fear. Touch my heart about the things You want me to act on, and give me the heart to love others like You do.

When the world seems so unjust to me, Lord, remind me that it treated You the same way. Shift my focus away from myself. Show me ways to help others whose situation is far worse than mine.

◇◇◇

Father, teach me to practice justice in even the smallest areas of my life. Reveal to me the truth of my actions. Help me to see that the choices I make affect the lives of others.

◇◇◇

Lord, true justice flows from Your heart and character. You want my faith in You to be marked by my concern for the things that matter to You—seeking the lost, freeing the oppressed, helping the helpless. I'm up against systems and institutions and policies that are too big and powerful for me, but You've called me to stand in Your strength, using Your tools. Help me to live by these words from the apostle Paul: "The world is unprincipled. It's dog-eat-dog out there! The world doesn't fight fair. But we don't live or fight our battles that way—never have and never will. The tools of our trade aren't for marketing or manipulation, but they are for demolishing that entire massively corrupt culture. We use our powerful God-tools for smashing warped philosophies, tearing down barriers erected against the truth of God, fitting every loose thought and emotion and impulse into the structure of life shaped by Christ. Our tools are ready at hand for clearing the ground of every obstruction and building lives of obedience into maturity" (2 Corinthians 10:3–6 MSG).

INSOMNIA

He grants sleep to those he loves.
PSALM 127:2 NIV

Insomnia can be a terrible issue. It makes us tired and cranky. When we're tired, we're more likely to feel anxious or depressed, more easily angered, less patient. It becomes a vicious circle: the more upset and tense we become, the less we can sleep; the less we sleep, the more upset and tense we become. . . .

We may end up afraid to even go to bed because we don't want to face the frustration we feel when we lie there awake again. Anxiety overwhelms us. We feel helpless.

But God is with us, even when we lie awake night after night. He has compassion on our sleeplessness. His love never fails.

God, there is no shortage of things to worry about. So much of it centers on what I need to get to live a good life—getting enough to pay the bills, put food on the table, deal with medical conditions, advance at work—but it's possible that I've lost sight of all You have already given me and will continue to give me—abundant life, the Holy Spirit, an important ongoing mission, and the promise of heaven, for starters. Help me to focus on You now and leave the rest to You.

◇◇◇

Sovereign God, my mind is racing. Please slow my thoughts and bring a calm over me. As I lay here in bed, let my breathing fall in rhythm with Your Spirit. Let me sense Your nearness. Bring to my mind all the times You've protected me in the past. I know that I have nothing to fear because You watch over me.

◇◇◇

Lord, take away the worries that multiply in my mind when I lie awake. As each anxious thought overtakes me, let me turn it over to You. You tell me to cast my cares upon You because You care for me.

◇◇◇

Dear God, I want to lie down and sleep in peace. I want to believe that You will keep me safe (Psalm 4:8). Above all, I want to just close my eyes and fall asleep. Please grant me a good night's rest tonight, I pray.

◇◇◇

Father, tonight I give my insomnia to You. If I stay awake all night, then that's okay. I'll be comfortable here in my bed, resting in Your presence. I submit my thoughts to You. I dwell in Your peace, and I take refuge in Your presence.

Lord, I don't understand why I can't get to sleep. If I need to
clear my conscience of anything, please show me, whether it's
sin or bad decisions or anxiety or worry. Whatever it is,
I will confess it and repent of it, trusting Your promise
to hear and forgive me (1 John 1:9). If I'm guilty,
guide me in finding a way to make things right.

◇◇◇

God, I cry out to You. Sustain me. Lay me down to sleep.
Awake me again tomorrow, refreshed (Psalm 3:4–5).

◇◇◇

As a child, I would pray, "Now I lay me down to sleep."
Lately, sleep does not come easily. I find myself tossing and
turning. By the time I fall asleep, it's almost time to get up
again. Father, I need You to help me. Give me peaceful sleep,
I pray. Just as I slept as a child, without a care in the world.

◇◇◇

Father, I need Your peace to guard my heart and mind
(Philippians 4:7). I need You to help control my emotions.
They spin out of control when I'm tired. Help me to sleep.
Restful sleep makes such a difference in my ability to face daily
trials. I'm a better spouse and parent when I get my sleep.
Please allow me to find peace and to sleep well
tonight when my head hits the pillow.

◇◇◇

God, insomnia is common. Help me to remember that this
is not unusual and that normally, with time, it will pass.
Many people struggle with it. I am not alone. In the hours
when I can't sleep, please remind me to use the time to pray.
I've been blessed in some of those quiet prayer times
spent with You while everyone else in the house is asleep.

Dear God, You know how my insomnia makes me suffer.
I have prayed for Your help and healing—but You haven't
seemed to answer. Teach my spirit to be still in the
quiet moments of the night when I cannot sleep.
Remind me to use this time for prayer.

◇◇◇

Loving Father, fill my heart with peace tonight.
May I relax in Your presence.

◇◇◇

Jesus, I ask for Your peace tonight. Your Word says to be
"anxious for nothing, but in everything by prayer and
supplication, with thanksgiving, let your requests be made
known to God" (Philippians 4:6 NKJV). I will think of things that
are noble, just, true, pure, lovely, of good report, virtuous, and
praiseworthy (v. 8). You are the God who never sleeps (Psalm
121:4). Guard my heart and mind with thoughts of You.

◇◇◇

Dearest God, as I lie here in bed, may I feel the echo of Your
Spirit's breath in my own breathing. May the peace of Your
presence lie over me like a blanket. May I recall all the things
You have done for me over the years. Help me to rest.

◇◇◇

Lord, take away the worries that plague me when I
lie awake. As each new anxiety rises to the surface
of my thoughts, help me to turn it over to You.

◇◇◇

Lord God, You are my protector, "a shield around me"
(Psalm 3:3 NIV). I have a million reasons not to sleep
tonight, and only one reason to rest: You.

ISOLATION AND LONELINESS

And I will pray the Father, and he shall give you another Comforter, that he may abide with you for ever; even the Spirit of truth. . . for he dwelleth with you, and shall be in you.

JOHN 14:16–17 KJV

Friends and family can offer precious support and comfort during dark days—but sometimes we must deal with a difficult time alone. No one else can stand in our shoes and experience exactly what we are experiencing. No matter how much we love each other, we can't fully understand each other's feelings—and that fact can seem like a wall that separates us from the ones we love the most.

But in our loneliness, we are never truly alone. The Comforter is with us. When no one else can take away our loneliness, the Holy Spirit is constantly present, speaking words of love that are for our ears alone.

Lord, I feel so lonely. Thank You that You're here with me.
I'm counting on You in a way I never have before.

◇◇◇

What can separate me from Your love, Christ? Can troubles or
pain or danger or illness? No, I know that in all these things
You are with me. For I am sure that neither death nor life, nor
angels nor rulers, nor things present nor things to come, nor
powers, nor height nor depth, nor anything else in all creation
will be able to separate me from the love of God in You,
Christ Jesus my Lord. (Romans 8:35–39)

◇◇◇

Jesus, when I read about Your death on the cross, I can tell You felt
forsaken. You felt death's horror. And yet in the midst of all that,
You still trusted Your Father. Help me to follow Your example.

◇◇◇

Lord, I'm realizing that when I reach the point where I have
nothing left but You, I can finally realize that. You are the
strength of my heart and my portion forever (Psalm 73:26).

◇◇◇

Blessed be You, God, for You are the Father of mercies.
You comfort me in my affliction, including this loneliness.
Use me to comfort those who are going through
something similar. (2 Corinthians 1:3–4)

◇◇◇

Even my closest friends don't understand what I'm going
through, Lord. But You do. Your grace never fails me.

◇◇◇

Lord, I believe You are here with me, going through this
at my side. You will be with me; You will not leave
me or forsake me (Deuteronomy 31:8).

JEALOUSY

The acts of the flesh are obvious: sexual immorality, impurity and debauchery; idolatry and witchcraft; hatred, discord, jealousy, fits of rage, selfish ambition, dissensions, factions and envy; drunkenness, orgies, and the like. I warn you, as I did before, that those who live like this will not inherit the kingdom of God.

GALATIANS 5:19–21 NIV

One of the first words a little child speaks is "mine." We are quick to announce what belongs to us and perhaps even quicker to want what is not! Like one toddler grabbing another's toy is the adult who gazes upon what friends have in envy.

Are you struggling with jealousy? It's subtle at first, but left unattended can overtake your entire life.

When you feel that little green monster creeping into your thoughts, say a prayer. Tell God that you're thankful for your friend, and ask Him to give you a heart that celebrates that friend's victories and accomplishments.

As I look at others, God, I admit that I'm sometimes envious. I look at their lives and find myself wanting what they have when I should appreciate my own blessings. Keep me focused on the positives in my life, the things others may long for that I have been given. These may be things I take for granted that others would love to have. Replace my envy with a heart of gratitude, I pray.

◇◇◇

God, I remember the story of Joseph and his colorful coat. Joseph's brothers were jealous of him and sold him into slavery. You were with Him through it all and You rescued him. You showed him favor and gave him great wisdom. You raised him up as a leader in Egypt in spite of his brothers' intentions (Acts 7:9–10). Work in my life too, Father. I'm being mistreated because of someone's jealousy. It's out of my control, but nothing is out of Your control. I ask You to work on my behalf.

◇◇◇

Father, I know that You are a jealous God. You desire that I have no other gods above You. Where am I spending most of my time and money? These may be areas of my life that need close examination. Please help me to eliminate anything that threatens to become a god in my life.

Lord, You know the desires of my heart. Help me to be happy for others when they are successful or receive blessings or rewards. Just because all the longings in my own life are not yet fulfilled, I don't want to be bitter about others' victories. Help me, Father, as I struggle with jealousy.

◇◇◇

I remember the old song that offers this advice: "Count your blessings. Name them one by one. Count your many blessings. See what God has done!" There is no time like the present for me to stop and do just this. Thank You, Father, for each of these blessings in my life. Thank You for [list the blessings in your life]. I am so very blessed.

◇◇◇

God, I see my girlfriends' families on social media. They all look so perfect and happy. Meanwhile, my own is struggling. I see their profile pictures. They seem so pretty and put-together. I never look like that! I've gained weight, and I'm looking older these days. It's so easy for me to compare myself to others. Please help me to realize that while my life is not perfect, neither are theirs! Help me not to grow jealous of my friends but to pray for them and to recognize the blessings in my life.

JOB LOSS

Wealth from hard work grows over time.
PROVERBS 13:11 NLT

◇

Losing a job is a painful experience. We look to our jobs for status and security. Without them, our identities may seem less certain, less valuable even. We are filled with anxiety for the future. Now that this calamity has come upon us, we worry that even worse things lie ahead. How will we be able to pay our bills? Will we lose our house? What if we end up homeless and on the street?

But God is with us in these circumstances, just as He always was. He asks us to be patient. He assures us that if we are willing to work hard, we will have financial security once more. And He promises He is still working in our lives.

I don't know what You are doing by allowing this to happen, but I trust You to help provide for me and my family while this season endures. I commit to keeping my eyes on You, giving You everything I'm feeling, and expecting You to make something good out of this. I need You more than ever.

◇◇◇

Lord, You know this time of unemployment is not what I had hoped for. But let me use it nevertheless to grow and rest and be useful to others. Help me to use this time wisely.

◇◇◇

Give me wisdom to manage my finances, Father. Show me how to adjust my lifestyle to these new circumstances. Remind me that all I truly need to be happy is Your presence.

◇◇◇

Lead me to a new job, I pray, dear Lord. Show me where to look. I thank You for the new people and new opportunities that lie ahead.

◇◇◇

Father, even in this time of loss, I have so much to thank You for— beginning with Jesus Christ, my Savior. Jesus died for me before I was even born, but You knew me even then, knew the blessings You would give me, and knew the challenges You would allow to help me depend on Your provision. Even though I liked my job, I love You more. I know You will take care of me and my family.

◇◇◇

Do I have any skills I've been overlooking, Lord? Is there something new You want me to be open to doing? Make this an opportunity for me to grow.

I don't know where to turn for help, Jesus. Show me people who are willing and able to guide me. Teach me how to network!

◇◇◇

Father, thank You that You have a plan for me. Even when I can't see what it is, lead me one step at a time.

◇◇◇

God, I've started to see how much value I put on the job I've lost. I've wondered how this could be Your plan for me. But I understand that Your ways and thoughts are higher than mine (Isaiah 55:8–9), and I'm beginning to grasp that this is part of what You meant when You said you are working "all things" together for my good. I want to get on board with what You're doing and learn what You're trying to teach me during this downtime. My worth is not in my work but in You.

◇◇◇

Take my hands, God, and use them for whatever work You want me to do. Take my feet, God, and lead me to the job openings where You want me to apply. Take my voice, God, and during each job interview, give me the words You want me to say. Take my eyes, God, and teach them to search for the job opportunities You want me to see. Take my mind, God, and give me the new ideas You want me to consider. Take my soul, God, and fill me with Your Spirit in a new way during this time of unemployment. Take my life, God, and whether I have a job or am unemployed, use me for the purposes of Your heart.

◇◇◇

My family needs me to lead them spiritually, even if I'm not providing financially. This is one of the hardest things I've ever been through, but I choose to do it in a way that honors You.

JOB STRESS

Work willingly at whatever you do, as though you were working for the Lord rather than for people.
COLOSSIANS 3:23 NLT

Our jobs are often the source of much of the stress in our lives. Tight deadlines, multiple responsibilities, conflicts with coworkers and supervisors—all these can lead to tension. We're likely to spend about half our lives in our workplaces, though, so we need to find joy and satisfaction, rather than stress and anxiety, in our jobs.

We can learn to sense God's presence with us as we work. Even on our busiest days, we need to take time to whisper a prayer or spend a quiet moment with our Lord.

God, work is so stressful right now that I can't think straight.
I want to follow Your priorities, no matter what's going on at
work. If my work feels meaningless, You can give meaning to
what I do when I do it for You. If I place too much of my self-
worth on my job, help me find my true identity in You as the
child You love and a servant working toward kingdom goals.
I will keep perspective on the chaos at work by reminding
myself that everything I do is to be done ultimately for You.

◇◇◇

God, thank You for my career. Thank You for giving me a job
that I enjoy and one that suits my gifts. Help me to find
a balance, though, between work and home. I don't want
my family to suffer because I'm stressed out about work.

◇◇◇

May the words of my mouth be pleasing to You. I struggle with
this. When I'm tired and stressed, I often fail to speak to my
employer or my employees in a way that honors You, God.
Help me to take a deep breath in those times and whisper
a prayer. Help me to remember that my tongue has the
power to lift others up or tear them down. I want to
honor You with how I speak in my workplace.

◇◇◇

Jesus, You're my real boss. You love me, You're for me,
and You understand me (Colossians 3:23–24). I want Your
priorities and values to inform how I operate at work. As Your
representative, I commit to being the best worker I can be—
diligent, prompt, reliable, organized, and relational—and to
seeking the highest good of the people with whom I work.
Guide me as I face difficult situations and relationships at work.

I come before You, Lord, and I admit I'm not in a very good state. I'm stressed out and overworked and tired, so tired. It's in moments such as these that I refocus. I find You there. You never moved. It was I who drifted. I look up and find my Father's face smiling down at me. You offer me an easy yoke. I accept, Abba Father. I will rest in You.

◇◇◇

At times I feel like everyone and everything is against me. I can't please my employer no matter how many hours I put in or how hard I work. Remind me, Lord, that You are for me. If You are for me, who can be against me? (Romans 8:31).

◇◇◇

God, lead me today. May I serve You as I work. Thank You for the opportunity to do this job. May I do it for You, as a labor of love.

◇◇◇

Lord Jesus, as I enter this workplace, I bring Your presence with me. May I speak Your peace and grace to everyone with whom I interact today. I acknowledge Your lordship over all that will be said and done today.

◇◇◇

Lord, I realize that a lot of my stress at work comes from not taking time to rest and recharge. Forgive me for not observing any kind of a Sabbath—a rest period where I just slow down, shift gears, and trust You to provide the energy and ability to do what needs to be done when I go back to work. I will be deliberate about taking time off to recharge.

◇◇◇

Be with each of my interactions today. May others see You in me.

Thank You, loving Lord, for the gifts You have given me. Help me to use them responsibly and well today as I do my work. Anoint my creativity, my ideas, and my energy, so that even the smallest tasks will bring Your light to the world.

◇◇◇

Father, work has been extra stressful recently. There are different reasons for it, but I want to keep my eyes on You. I don't want to respond to stress by complaining, speaking in anger, or coping in unhealthy ways like eating junk food, drinking, or binge-watching TV. I'm grateful that You have given me a job, and I want to honor You by doing it the best I can. The way I handle hardship is part of my witness (2 Corinthians 12:8–10). You're the One I don't want to disappoint.

◇◇◇

Heavenly Lord, thank You for my job. May I be challenged and inspired by the work I do. Even in the midst of stress, even on the days when I fail, may I look away from my own feelings and see You—as well as a world that needs my efforts, no matter how small they may seem. Give me the will and strength to work hard today. May I find gladness in my efforts, and most of all, may I please You.

God, I feel so torn. I want to be the best at everything, but so often, due to overload and stress, I feel I'm letting everyone down. My spouse, my children, my boss, and my coworkers. Show me how to balance my time. Remind me that often the work can wait and needs to be laid down at a certain time so that my family life does not take second place.

◇◇◇

Lord, I want to handle my job stress in ways that please You. While I would love to do work that allows me to use the gifts and talents You've given me, I trust that You can still use me in positive ways in my current job. Keep my focus on the opportunity You've given me to provide for me and my family. Help me to recognize all the personal, petty, political quarrels that people get into at work and to avoid them. I don't know if it's possible for me to truly enjoy this job, but I know that nothing is impossible for You. As long as You have me there, I will look to honor You with my work.

◇◇◇

Father, when I am confused at work, guide me. When I am weary, energize me. When I am burned out, shine the light of Your Holy Spirit on me.

LEADERSHIP

Be diligent to present yourself approved to God, a worker who does not need to be ashamed, rightly dividing the word of truth.
2 TIMOTHY 2:15 NKJV

◆

Here is a simple but profound truth: you are a leader. You may think you're not, but if you are a Christian, God has called you to follow Christ and to lead others to Him. No matter who you are or where you work, you're a leader. Even if you're not the head of a household, you're a leader. If you don't have a college degree or a ton of work experience, you're still a leader. That's because God has called you as a believer to join in His work, the family business of sharing the Gospel and making disciples.

Following Jesus' example, you lead not by lording it over others but by getting low—by humbling yourself to serve in the best way you can. That starts by getting into God's Word daily and learning about Him and what matters to Him—and then putting it into practice.

You'll need to pray and be in fellowship with other like-minded Christians, because the more you learn about God, the more you learn about yourself—your strengths and weaknesses, and how to die to yourself so you can become more and more like Jesus. The kingdom of God needs you to embrace your leadership role, to avoid passivity, and to begin ministering where you are, right now.

Lord, I am tired of feeling ineffective and incapable of leadership. I want to accomplish Your purposes for my life and through my life in the lives of others. I want to model what it is to follow Christ, to humble myself and "go low" in prayer and service. I trust that You can use me right where I am.

◇◇◇

God, despite all I have accomplished at work, it seems like I have no real influence or credibility on a personal level. I want more—I want what You have for me. I need to put aside any instincts to control or compete or manipulate others to get what I want. I need to model integrity and righteousness, earning the right to instruct, and even confront, others by showing them that I care about them as people first.

◇◇◇

Father, I've invested so much time and energy into serving myself—building up my reputation and my résumé—that I've forgotten that I am to represent You in all I do and say. I've been shortsighted, lacking self-awareness and avoiding God-awareness. Forgive me.

◇◇◇

Lord, I realize that I have been passive in my leadership role. I'm beginning to see the cost of my inability and unwillingness to get involved or to confront problems or take stands on important issues. I've excused it as just being humble or meek, but I see that my version of those things is very different from Jesus' demonstration of those qualities. He told the truth—sometimes through stories, sometimes directly—but He always sought Your will and Your best in the lives of the people He encountered. Help me to love others like that, at home and at work.

LITIGATION

And thou shalt speak unto him, and put the words in his mouth: and I will be with thy mouth, and with his mouth, and will teach you what ye shall do.

EXODUS 4:15 ASV

Bringing lawsuits against each other has become commonplace in our world today. This is not necessarily a bad thing. It is certainly better to turn to the courts to settle a problem rather than use violence. We don't want to go back to the days of the Wild West, where the fastest gun ruled! It's unfortunate, however, that so many of today's conflicts are unable to be settled by people simply working out a compromise.

When litigation is filed against us, it's a stressful situation. We will feel afraid and angry. It is hard to know the right course of action to take.

But God will be with us! He will give us the words to say—and He will also be with the other side, the person who is taking us to court. His Holy Spirit doesn't take sides, and He always works for peace.

You know whether I have been justly named in this lawsuit.
I believe that I have not, and I plead my case before You.
Deliver me, according to Your righteous nature and judgment.
I hold on to Your Word: "The Lord will fight for you,
and you have only to be silent" (Exodus 14:14 ESV).

◇◇◇

Lord, as I face this legal battle, I clothe myself with Your
righteousness, integrity, and love. Thank You that You are
always present with me. Help me to be honest, both with myself
and with those who are taking me to court. Show me if I am at
fault. Free me from anger, hate, and the desire for revenge.

◇◇◇

Lord Jesus, I ask You that truth would prevail. Protect me from
those who tell lies about me. Reassure me that You are my
defense. May Your Spirit give me the right words to speak.

◇◇◇

Father, make me ready to forgive. Show us if there
is another option for settling this conflict.

◇◇◇

Jesus, You told us to come to terms quickly with our accusers
on our way to court (Matthew 5:25). I pray that You
would open the door to peace in this situation.

◇◇◇

Lead me to the right legal counsel, heavenly Father.
May my attorney give me advice that comes from You.

◇◇◇

Loving God, You promise that You do not hate me when
others accuse me. You will hear my cry. (Psalm 22:24)

Help me, Lord! You know how scared I am about this court case. Your Word tells me that You are just and You are my defense. Let me rely on You. Plead my cause. Deliver me from this crisis. Be my rock of refuge, my strong fortress in the midst of all this. Go before me and fight this battle on my behalf.

◇◇◇

Father, the pressure and uncertainty of this lawsuit is crushing my spirit and sickening my body. I am trying to represent You as I face it, but I believe the suit has no legal merit. Please get it dismissed in whatever way You choose. You are my strength and my shield (Psalm 28:7), and You have said that no weapon formed against me shall succeed (Isaiah 54:17).

◇◇◇

Lord, as I face this unjust lawsuit, Your Word gives me peace: "If anyone attacks you, don't for a moment suppose that I sent them, and if any should attack, nothing will come of it. I create the blacksmith who fires up his forge and makes a weapon designed to kill. I also create the destroyer—but no weapon that can hurt you has ever been forged. Any accuser who takes you to court will be dismissed as a liar. This is what GOD's servants can expect. I'll see to it that everything works out for the best" (Isaiah 54:15–17 MSG).

◇◇◇

Lord, my case is coming up and my stomach is tied in knots. Only You know whether I will go free or face punishment. I confess my sins before You, and I turn from them. I ask You to deliver me from this, Lord. I commit to being the person and citizen You have called me to be. I leave all this in Your hands, but pray that whether or not I go free, You would free me in Jesus Christ.

LONELINESS

My soul, wait in silence for God only, for my hope is from Him.
PSALM 62:5 NASB

If you're single, you may be lonely for a mate. If you have a mate, you may be lonely in your marriage. If you have children, you may be lonely when they're away or you may think of the days when you were unencumbered by motherly duties. You may miss running around with your girlfriends, footloose and fancy free. You may be lonely for those friends who don't come around much anymore now that you're changing diapers or driving the car pool. If you live alone, you may be lonely for companionship. If you live with others, you may be lonely even in their presence. Loneliness does not always mean alone. You may be painfully lonesome even in a crowd of people.

If you rely on a person to fill the God-shaped hole in your heart, you will find that the puzzle piece never quite fits. You'll remain lonely, and you'll grow tired of working aimlessly at filling the void.

Learn to seek God. Be still before your Maker, your Redeemer, your Best Friend.

He is the only one who can fill the lonely crevices of your soul.

When I call to You, You answer. When I am in trouble,
You come running. You are with me (Psalm 91:15).
That is such a comfort to me, God.

◇◇◇

Heavenly Father, he lies next to me in bed but I'm lonely.
He sits at the same dinner table with me, but I can't think
of things to say that will engage him. We've grown distant,
and I'm so lonely in my marriage. Please help us, Father.
Please help me to reach out. Show me how to
connect with my husband again, I pray.

◇◇◇

You will not leave me. You have called me by name. You call me
Your own. When I pass through deep waters, You will not let me
drown (Isaiah 43:1–5). Loneliness overwhelms me, but You are
still here with me. You never look away. You never wander.
You are my God, always near. For that I am so very thankful.

◇◇◇

Help me, Lord, to reach out to those who may be lonely today.
It often helps me to do something for others. There is always
someone worse off than me, someone I can minister
to, someone who could use a friend. Show me the
opportunities You have for me to be a light today.

God, I'm lonely. There are so many things I want to do, but often, I can't think of anyone who would want to go and do them with me. I long for a close friend. Please help me to find a new Christian friend. Remind me, Father, that even if I have hundreds of friends, I need You more than any other.

◇◇◇

This is a lonely season for me, Father. I remember a time when my life was full of people. Things have changed. I find myself alone more often. Use this season, Lord, to draw me closer to You. Let me fellowship with my Father when I'm alone. As a Christian, I'm never really alone, for You are always near. You will be with me always, even to the end of the age (Matthew 28:20).

◇◇◇

God, I'm busy all day with my children. My home and vehicle are filled with my own kids and their friends and classmates almost all the time. How can I still feel lonely? I think I miss adult conversations. I need friends in my life again. Thank You in advance, God, for helping me to find some time for me—outside of being Mommy.

MARITAL STRIFE/DYSFUNCTION

"So then, they are no longer two but one flesh. Therefore what God has joined together, let not man separate."
Matthew 19:6 NKJV

Conflict is a reality of marriage, even in the best relationships. That doesn't mean your marriage is doomed, although if you don't get to the core issues and work on resolving them, the bumpy parts of the ride can seem unending.

If either you or your spouse thought you were marrying a perfect person, you were entering marriage with your eyes half-shut. Before you got married, you probably found your differences complementary. Now, however, they've somehow become problematic. But it's not that either of you has suddenly swapped personalities; you've just changed your perspective, realizing that it's challenging to live day in and day out with another person.

Check your expectations. Are they realistic? Measure your behavior against Paul's instruction: "Let each one of you love his wife as himself, and let the wife see that she respects her husband" (Ephesians 5:33 ESV). Invite conversation instead of confrontation. Learn to live with each other with understanding and appreciation for the work God is doing in each of you—and how He is using each of you to teach the other to die to yourselves. God's design for marriage includes unique blessings of intimacy that mirror the profound depth of Christ's relationship with the church. It's worth fighting for.

God, You made me and my wife one flesh (Genesis 2:24)—joined in every way: emotionally, physically, spiritually, financially. But lately we can't seem to stop treating each other like the enemy. I feel disrespected, but I admit that I have not loved her like Christ loved the church. Forgive me, and make me into the husband You want her to have. Help us to find godly counsel and good friends with whom we can share our journey.

◇◇◇

Lord, Your Word says love "always protects, always trusts, always hopes, always perseveres" (1 Corinthians 13:7 NIV). You've called me to love my wife no matter how she responds, but I see that if I love her the way I'm supposed to, she is much more likely to respond in positive ways.

◇◇◇

Father, guide me in loving my wife the way You've called me to—sacrificially. Although she is my wife, she has always been Your daughter. I want to love her in a way that honors You. That includes fighting for her best interests because they are tied to mine. Keep chipping away at me so that more and more of You is revealed. Help us to learn and grow from those conflicts, becoming better off, not bitter.

◇◇◇

Father, we keep running into the same obstacles in our marriage and having the same kinds of fights. We trust that You have more for us, and that You can use each of us to smooth out the other's rough spots. My wife is worth fighting for.

God, please bless my marriage. I understand that when I draw closer to You, and my wife does the same, we grow closer together. Show me the negativity in my heart—anything that keeps me from showing patience, forgiveness, kindness, and affection toward my wife. Give me the wisdom I need to distinguish between faults and sins, and to strive for resolution when there's a conflict. Help me learn when to give way and when to hold the line. I commit to listening twice as much as I speak—and listening well. I commit to being responsible in my devotion to You, regularly spending time in Your Word and in prayer so I can know what kind of man You want me to be. Make my marriage like a full moon, like a beautiful reflection of the Son.

◇◇◇

Lord, Your Word says that a wife should submit to her husband "as to the Lord" (Ephesians 5:22 ESV). I confess, however, that I have used that verse to make demands of my wife but have conveniently ignored the verses close by on either side of it: "Husbands, love your wives, as Christ loved the church and gave himself up for her" (v. 25) and the call to be "submitting to one another out of reverence for Christ" (v. 21). So, I submit to You, asking You to help me love my wife like You love the church—giving up all I am for her and seeking to help her know You better. Forgive me, and help me to become the man she needs.

MOVING

"Remember that I commanded you to be strong and brave. Don't be afraid, because the Lord your God will be with you everywhere you go."
Joshua 1:9 NCV

Moving can be exciting, but often it brings at least some degree of difficulty and stress. You're leaving behind what you know and stepping into the unknown. Will you have friends in the new place? Will your neighbors be nice?

Even though the old house had its issues, you're used to its creaks and quirks. You'll miss them! There will be new and unfamiliar sounds in the new home. You're not sure you can adjust, but you will.

As you leave one place and head toward another, recognize that God goes with you. The house is just walls. God abides within your heart. He will dwell with you in any place that you may call home for the rest of your life. Embrace this move. Choose to step into change with confidence that your God has gone before you to prepare the way.

There is a time for everything. There is a season for everything that happens under heaven (Ecclesiastes 3:1). I loved our home, but this is the time to move. We made a lot of memories there. I'll miss some things about it, but I will not look back. I will look forward (Isaiah 43:18). You have moved us, and we are following You, God.

◇◇◇

My heart is torn, God. Part of me wants to stay, but the other part knows it's time to move on from this place. It's hard to step into the unknown, but I know that You go with me. Please prepare the way for me. I will walk in it. I choose to trust You in this move, Father.

◇◇◇

I remember when we moved into this house, God. It was new to us then. The rooms seemed empty and big. Gradually we filled up this place with children and stuff and more children and more stuff. It's so familiar now. I don't even need the light on to move from room to room in the night. This house has been a good home for us, and I'll miss it here. But You've called us to a new place. There will be empty rooms there, but we'll fill them up with "us." Soon it will feel like home. Soon I won't have this sick feeling in my stomach the way I do today as I say good-bye to our house.

God, I'm scared. I've resisted this move and dug in my heels, and even when the house sold easily and You provided the new one, I remained stubborn. There have been so many signs that this is Your will, but I'm just afraid. I need You to give me peace about this move, Father.

◇◇◇

I won't know the neighbors, Lord. I won't know where the closest post office is or the best dry cleaner to use. I'll have to change doctors and grocery stores, and the kids will have to start at a new school. So many changes, God, and change is not easy for us. Please hold us close.

◇◇◇

Help me to be positive about this move, Lord. Even though the circumstances are not ideal, help me to trust You. I need to be strong for others who are looking to me for their own strength in this move, God. Please give me a smile and a countenance that displays confidence that can come only from You.

OVERWHELMED

*The righteous cry out, and the LORD hears them;
he delivers them from all their troubles.*
PSALM 34:17 NIV

It's no wonder that people often feel overwhelmed in today's society. Many are juggling a job outside the home along with the duties of being a spouse and parent. Others are single parents who must balance a career with raising children on their own. Some have climbed the ladder in major corporations or built their own businesses, working far too many hours each day. Those who are older may be overwhelmed by the responsibility of raising grandchildren they never imagined they would be called on to raise.

Regardless of your circumstances, know that you can turn to God. He understands. He's ready to help you. Sometimes all we need is a good cry! God gets that. He's there to listen and to comfort you. Other times, we need to sort through the stress in our lives and make some necessary changes. Ask Him for guidance, and He will gladly show you the way.

I'm overwhelmed today, God. You've seen my to-do list! Something needs to give, but I don't know where to make the changes. It seems that everything is equally important. I have to work so that my family can have income, but I have to be there for my kids or they'll feel I don't love them. Show me the way. I ask this in Jesus' name.

◇◇◇

I come to You. I am burdened and weary. I need the rest that can only be found in You, Jesus (Matthew 11:28).

◇◇◇

When I'm overwhelmed, You are the One who knows the way I should turn (Psalm 142:3). Show me, Father. I'm ready to make some changes to reduce the stress in my life.

◇◇◇

I'm so overwhelmed by all of life's demands on me. Before I begin my work, I'll stop and spend time with You. I choose to put You first. I choose to rest in You so that You will bless the labor of my hands. I need You, God.

◇◇◇

I remember a demonstration where a jar was filled with sand and then rocks were added. All of the rocks would not fit. But when the rocks were put in first, the sand was poured in and everything easily fit into the jar. God, help me to get my priorities straight. If I spend time with You first thing each morning, the rest of my day will flow much more smoothly, and You will multiply my time that I might do all that I need to do.

When You return, I want to be busy about Your kingdom work. I don't want to be snowed under beneath a pile of work and deadlines. I don't want to tell You, "But Jesus, I wasn't ready for You yet. I have too much to do. I'm so busy. Can You return another day? I need a bit more time." Help me to live each day as if it were the day You were returning for me. I will live differently if I keep my sights set on that day!

◇◇◇

God, my husband and kids don't seem to care. They hear me say how overwhelmed I am, and yet they continue to ask more and more of me. I need a break. I need help. Show me ways that I can delegate some of the chores. Show me how to confront my family and insist on their help without being mean-spirited. I can't do all of this on my own. I really need them, God.

PHYSICAL PAIN

*Be very glad—for these trials make you partners
with Christ in his suffering.*
1 PETER 4:13 NLT

Jesus experienced pain. He did not hold Himself separate from human experience, and He died on the cross in terrible agony. This means that He understands what we feel when we face emotional and physical pain. We can turn to Him, knowing that even if no one else understands what we are going through, He truly understands.

Even more than that, through pain we can come to know Jesus better. As we allow His Spirit to work in us, we become partners with Him in a new way, sharing in His suffering on the cross.

God, this pain has taken control of my life. I feel weak and helpless. Discouragement, frustration, and resentment threaten to drown me. Lord, please show me the way forward. Allow me to find ways to control this pain. Teach me how to live with it. Transform it into something that leads me closer to You, I pray in Your name.

◇◇◇

Jesus, I feel as though I can't take this pain anymore. It takes all my energy to handle it, leaving me so little energy for anything else. Please anoint me with Your strength. I surrender this pain to You. Please carry it when I am too weak— and if it be Your will, please take it from me.

◇◇◇

Jesus, I don't know how to obey when the apostle Paul tells us to rejoice in our sufferings. I will wait on You, though, believing that somehow this suffering will produce endurance. . .and endurance will produce strength of character. . .and that hope will grow out of that, a hope that will never be disappointed. Thank You for pouring Your love into my heart through the Holy Spirit. (Romans 5:3–5)

Heavenly Father, please touch the area of discomfort and
bring relief. Release the muscles that are tight, and bring
Your restoration. May the pain retreat enough
that sleep will be peaceful.

◇◇◇

Lord, this constant pain is a heavy burden.
I cast it on You. Sustain me, I pray (Psalm 119:116).

◇◇◇

Almighty God, You are the Creator, the Master Builder, the
One who shaped our bodies before we were born. You breathe
life into each cell and hold everything in place. Your Spirit lives
in our earthly bodies. I ask now for Your Holy Spirit to move
in this physical body. Bring relief from pain, I pray.
Be Lord of this body and ease its discomforts.

◇◇◇

You are our Savior, Jesus, who came to this earth to be with us
in all our pain. Thank You that You are here now and that
You are carrying this pain too. Use this pain to draw
me closer to You. May I learn to see pain as
a way to share Your work on the cross.

PHYSICAL WEAKNESS

But those who trust in the Lord will find new strength. They will soar high on wings like eagles. They will run and not grow weary. They will walk and not faint.
ISAIAH 40:31 NLT

Physical weakness is hard to bear. We want to be *better*. We want our old lives back. We want our bodies to be the way they used to be, capable of doing all that they once did. We have days when we ask ourselves, "How much further can I go? How much longer can I keep on like this?" Days like that, we long to give up. We feel too weak to keep going.

All we can do now is turn again to the Lord, trusting that He will give us new strength—not only to walk through our days without fainting but also to soar on eagles' wings. When we acknowledge our own weakness, that's the moment when the Holy Spirit can begin to work in our lives in new ways.

Lord, You know how weak I am. But I can do all things through You because You give me strength (Philippians 4:13).

◇◇◇

Heavenly Father, make me strong in You. May my strength come from Your might (Ephesians 6:10).

◇◇◇

Jesus, I'm so weak, so exhausted. I'm not sure I can go on. I just want to give up. So take over. Do for me what I'm too weak to do for myself.

◇◇◇

God, the Bible says that a merry heart will do me good (Proverbs 17:22). Give me reasons to laugh today, I pray.

◇◇◇

Jesus, You know that my spirit is willing, but my flesh is weak. Remind me to keep watching and praying (Matthew 26:41).

◇◇◇

If by faith Sarah was able to have a baby, even when she was old (Hebrews 11:11), Lord God, I believe You can also work miracles in my body. Put new life in me that I may serve You once again.

◇◇◇

Spirit of Truth, I know You satisfy those who are weary and refresh everyone who is weak (Jeremiah 31:25). Come to my aid now, I pray.

PORNOGRAPHY

Run from sexual sin! No other sin so clearly affects the body as this one does. For sexual immorality is a sin against your own body.

1 Corinthians 6:18 NLT

Erotic images make us feel powerful and in control, but these sensations are fleeting and false. Porn is like a gateway drug that causes hormones in key areas of your brain—areas God intended for pleasure with your wife—to be dispersed among a panorama of images, numbing the sensations so that the regular viewer must constantly seek more lurid content to get the same "high." It's a self-made trap.

But God has provided a way out. It begins with repentance—turning away from your porn habit. This may mean getting filters for your devices or even abandoning the internet if need be. It means disciplining yourself in studying God's Word, renewing your mind (Romans 12:1–2). Every time you feel like viewing the bad stuff, go to the Bible instead and fill your mind with the good stuff. Finally, you need accountability. This is the hardest part for most guys, but it's important to bring your private life into the light. Find at least one other male believer and tell him about your porn use. Have him check in with you regularly (maybe daily at first, then weekly). If you're serious about breaking free from lust, God will use these practices to liberate you.

God, thank You that Your Word says that "he who does the will of God abides forever" (1 John 2:17 NKJV). I have sought my own will, my own pleasure, for far too long, and I can feel the distance it has created between me and You. As I seek You in prayer and in Your Word, deliver me from pornography's grip and from the lust of my heart. You are stronger than my sin.

◇◇◇

Pierce my darkness, Lord. Turn my eyes toward You, Your Word and ways, so that I can win the battle in my mind's eye.

◇◇◇

Lord, my porn use has damaged intimacy between me and my wife. I've objectified women for my own pleasure for so long that I have forgotten what it means to share real intimacy with the one woman You intended for me to be with. Help me as I confess my sin to her and seek help to get us back on the right path.

◇◇◇

Father, meet me in the midst of my failure. I've tried to stay pure and have fallen again. The weight of my sin is especially heavy right now. I don't understand how You can keep loving me when I hate myself so much. I'm desperate for relief. Get this out of me! Your Word reminds me that "godly grief produces a repentance that leads to salvation without regret, whereas worldly grief produces death" (2 Corinthians 7:10 ESV).

PRAISE IN THE MIDST OF THE WORST

GOD is good, a hiding place in tough times. He recognizes and welcomes anyone looking for help, no matter how desperate the trouble.
NAHUM 1:7 MSG

Coping with difficult life situations isn't easy. But as you get used to a new reality, you'll find that God is still bringing joy into your life. There will still be things that give you pleasure. Safe in God's hiding place, you can appreciate life's small pleasures: a beautiful sunrise, a child's smile, a friend's laughter. And no matter how desperate you feel at times, there are still so many reasons to praise God. The love others share with you takes on new meaning. You may even discover a new sense of purpose. God is waiting to bless you—so that you can praise Him even now.

I praise You, Lord, with all my soul. With all my inmost being,
I praise Your holy name, I praise You, and I remember everything
You have done for me. You forgave me, You redeemed me,
You crowned me with love and compassion. You satisfy my
desires with good things so that my youth is
renewed like the eagle's. (Psalm 103:1–5)

◇◇◇

I shout for joy to You, Lord. I worship You with gladness.
I come before You with joyful songs. I know that You are God.
You made me, and I am Yours. I am part of Your people,
the sheep of Your pasture. I enter Your gates with thanksgiving
and Your courts with praise. I give thanks to You and I
praise Your name, even now. For You are good
and Your love endures forever. (Psalm 100)

◇◇◇

Your love, Jesus, is as wide as the oceans, as deep as the sea,
and as tall as the heavens. I praise You! You are the Lord of life!
I hear You in the falling rain; I see You in the starry sky;
I feel You in the warmth of the sun on my face.
In each of these things, I give You praise.

◇◇◇

Today, dear God, You blessed me. Let me take some time
now to tell You how grateful I am. As I think back through
my day, remind me of each joy, both big and small.
Help me to see all that is still good in my life.

◇◇◇

"LORD, you are my God; I will exalt you and praise your name,
for in perfect faithfulness you have done wonderful
things, things planned long ago" (Isaiah 25:1 NIV).

PRODIGAL CHILDREN

"All your children will be taught by the LORD, and great will be their peace."
ISAIAH 54:13 NIV

There are few things that hurt quite so much as children who go astray. We long to run after them and bring them home—and yet we must respect their decisions. We ache to care for them and protect them the way we did when they were small—but they have gone beyond our protection. We feel so helpless.

But even when our children were babies, they were never truly ours. They always belonged to God. His hands held them. Only He kept them safe. And none of that has changed. Even now, if I have to sit back and watch as our children seem to run headlong toward danger, we can trust them to God's love. He is teaching them. He is shielding them. In the midst of what looks to us like chaos and confusion, He is there, leading our children into His peace.

Lord God, sometimes I feel like I'm trapped in a prison with my family. We're prisoners of bad choices and crushing consequences, but I pray that I would be able to lead us, even as we're in this dark place. Let Paul's words inspire and comfort me: "I am suffering here in prison. But I am not ashamed of it, for I know the one in whom I trust, and I am sure that he is able to guard what I have entrusted to him until the day of his return" (2 Timothy 1:12 NLT). I won't give up because You won't.

◇◇◇

My heart feels broken, Father. I know You understand, for You too must be heartsick when You watch Your children choose paths that lead them toward brokenness and sorrow. Heal my children, I pray, Lord. Lead them in Your paths. I gave them to You when they were small—and now I give them to You again.

◇◇◇

How am I to blame, Lord? I search the past for the answers. I agonize over my many mistakes. I long to go back and redo portions of my life. I am so sorry for the times I failed my children! But Father, I know that only You are perfect.
Work in my children's lives, despite my failures.
Use even my mistakes to bring them closer to You.

◇◇◇

I look back with rose-colored glasses, but I know there were some rough times as I was bringing up my children. I was far from the perfect parent. Please forgive me for the times I failed them, God. Please draw us back together. I miss them so.

Jesus, You told the story of the prodigal son. I imagine the father holding his tongue, fighting the urge to tell his son what a terrible mistake he was making. He let him go. Give me the grace to let my children go their own way. They're adults now and must make their own decisions.

◇◇◇

God, I feel like my children have changed but I haven't. Despite the way we raised our kids, the world got its teeth into them, and it feels like they've been poisoned against us and, worse yet, against You. I want to learn whatever it is You're trying to teach me as I deal with my children's choices. I love them and want Your best for them. Help me to love them like You do.

◇◇◇

God, I want to do something. I've always been a mover and a shaker. In this situation, I can't take control. I can't make things happen. I just have to pray. Help me never tire of praying for my children. There is great power in prayer. Remind me not to see it as a last resort. Keep me diligent in prayer and consistent in hope.

◇◇◇

What Joseph's brothers meant for evil, You used for good. You can use my child's choices. They seem wrong to me, but I must trust You with this child of mine. You work all things together for good in the lives of those who love You.

◇◇◇

Heavenly Father, my children know Your voice. I taught them about You and took them to church. They know the Bible and its truths. Your sheep know the sound of Your voice. Guide these little ones back to Your ways, Good Shepherd. I ask that You call out to them. I pray that they will heed Your call.

Jesus, in the story You told about the prodigal son, the father had the love and courage to let his child go. I ask that You give me the strength to do the same. Remind me not to lecture or nag. May I not judge. Give me grace to keep my mouth shut—and my heart open.

◇◇◇

I feel so helpless to do anything to help my child, Lord. Remind me that prayer is never the least I can do. It is always the most. May I never grow tired of praying for my child.

◇◇◇

Father, I thought I was raising arrows to shoot out into the world for Your glory, but I can't even keep them in the quiver properly (Psalm 127:3–5). Even so, Your Word in Habakkuk 3:17–18 points to my relationship with You as my strength when it feels like my family is coming apart at the seams. I will rejoice in You, even when there is little or no evidence of fruit in my children's lives. Lead me so I can know how to love them.

◇◇◇

Let my family see me walking with You through all this, learning and growing and relying on You. I will look for the good in my kids even when the bad is right in my face. Keep all our hearts tender toward You and each other.

◇◇◇

God, I affirm that You know best what my children need. I let my children go. The way they have chosen seems wrong to me. But that's between them and You. I will trust Your Holy Spirit to work in their lives and hearts, leading them into truth. No matter how many times I forget, remind me once again to step back and give You room to work!

This child is Yours, God. You blessed me with her and I gave her back to You. I trusted You with her all these years. Why would I try to take her back now? You know my daughter better than I do, better than she even knows herself. Please protect her. Please lead her back to the right path.

◇◇◇

Father, give me patience to wait. I want my children's situation to be different now! I long for things to "get back to normal." I know I sometimes pressure my children to move faster in the direction I wish they would go. Help me to trust Your timing in their lives.

◇◇◇

Father, please preserve my children as they stray from You. Don't hold against them whatever sins of mine have contributed to their distance from You. Protect them from the worst consequences of their own decisions. I know they will have regrets—I always have when I've strayed from You. At the same time, You have always been faithful to teach me more about Your grace, peace, and love through my mistakes. Please do the same with them. Let me be like the father of the prodigal son, who seemingly kept looking down the road in hopes that he would see his son coming home. When that day comes, I will rejoice!

REGRET

Brothers and sisters, I do not consider myself yet to have taken hold of it. But one thing I do: Forgetting what is behind and straining toward what is ahead.
PHILIPPIANS 3:13 NIV

The apostle Paul who penned these words in a letter to the Philippians had a sordid past. He'd been a killer of Christians. Looking back would do nothing but bring him deep regret and sorrow. He had no time for such things. He was about kingdom work. He was preaching the Gospel and spreading the good news of Jesus.

If you have asked God to forgive you, He has done so. It's as simple as that. You're a clean slate. Now turn from the past, go toward your future, and let God write on that slate as He will. Commit yourself today to focusing on Jesus and you will find that the troubling regrets you've been carrying will fade away. As the famous hymn goes, *"Turn your eyes upon Jesus. Look full in His wonderful face. And the things of earth will grow strangely dim in the light of His glory and grace."*

God, I keep looking back. I know You've forgiven me, but I'm struggling to forgive myself. This sin seems bigger than others. It seems like something I should pay for and keep paying for the rest of my life. Help me to accept that Jesus paid the debt for all my sin and that I'm forgiven and loved. I am a new creation in Him.

◇◇◇

I've broken one of Your commandments, O Lord. I have not been a godly person. No one knows the secret I bear. But You know. It burns within me, and I feel like maybe it would help to tell someone. Please guide me to a trusted person if this truly would help me. I'm filled with regret, and I wish I could go back in time and change things. I can't. Please hold me close, Father. I feel so undeserving of Your love today.

◇◇◇

If I confess my sins, You are faithful to forgive and cleanse me of all unrighteousness (1 John 1:9). I don't have to live with regret. It's a burden You desire for me to lay down at Your feet. Help me to do just that, God, and give me the strength to move on rather than pick it up again.

Give me a glad heart, Lord Jesus. A glad heart makes a cheerful face (Proverbs 15:13). I've been weighed down far too long with sorrow. My spirit has been crushed by this deep regret over what I've done. I long to be happy once again.

◇◇◇

I look to You, Sovereign God. I trade a countenance that reflects regret for one that shines with the radiance of my God (Psalm 34:5). I am forgiven and free.

◇◇◇

I'm deeply sorry for the way things turned out. I wish I could turn back the hands of time and change my actions and hold my tongue. I wish I could make different choices. I wish. . .but wishing can go on and on, and still nothing changes. I heard it said once that if we spend too much time dwelling on the past, we will miss the present and have no future. I don't want that to be me, God! Help me to release the past and take hold of the future that You have in store for me. I want to be used in a mighty way for Your kingdom.

SELF-ESTEEM

Therefore, there is now no condemnation for those who are in Christ Jesus.
ROMANS 8:1 NIV

◊

You are precious to your heavenly Father. He created Adam and Eve in His image, and He created you. He chose you as His beloved child. He saved your soul, watching His only Son, Jesus, die upon the cross to do so.

You could not be more loved. He loves you unconditionally on your best days, and on your worst exactly the same. He's not measuring your value according to your outward appearance, the amount of money in your account, or the type of clothing you wear. He's not counting the number of "likes" you receive on social media or the number of friends who click on your profile each day.

You are your God's pride and joy. You are His masterpiece. One day He will gather you to Himself in heaven. Jesus has gone there to prepare a special place for you. For today, surrender your troubles with self-esteem to Him. You are fully loved, and you need no other to love you. You belong to the God of the universe. He hugs His child close and says to call Him *Abba,* which means "daddy." Find your worth in Him and in Him alone.

God, I want to trade my low self-esteem for Christ-esteem. Make me confident in who I am through Christ. I wrestle with dark spiritual powers of evil, but You are greater than these (Ephesians 6:12). Remind me of my salvation and of my great worth in Christ Jesus.

◇◇◇

Father, I'm not sure what's causing me to feel so poorly about myself. Please examine my heart and reveal to me the ways my attitudes about myself need to change. I want to be a confident follower of God who is free to share Christ with those around me.

◇◇◇

You knit me together in my mother's womb. I am fearfully and wonderfully made. Wonderful are Your works, Creator God (Psalm 139:13–14).

◇◇◇

God, You don't look at the outward appearance but at the heart. You are not concerned with my height or weight. You don't see as humans see. You see who I am on the inside. Remind me that my heart is what matters most. Thank You for loving me the way You do, Lord.

There is so much pressure in society for me to look and dress a certain way. I just can't keep up! God, You tell us in Your Word that our adorning should be the hidden person that I am in my heart—a gentle and quiet spirit, which is precious in Your sight (1 Peter 3:3–4). Remind me that outward appearance is not all it's cracked up to be!

◇◇◇

You know the number of hairs on my head (Luke 12:7). You created me in Your image (Genesis 1:27). Charm is deceptive and beauty is vain, but a woman who fears the Lord is to be praised (Proverbs 31:30).

◇◇◇

I look around at my friends and my spouse and even my own children. They all seem to have such wonderful gifts and abilities. What is mine? I know that I do a lot to help others, but I sometimes wish I had a captivating singing voice or a great talent in sports or the arts. Father, help me to find my gifts and to use them for Your glory. And help me to remember that I am of great value to You (Matthew 10:31).

SEXUAL IDENTITY

So now there is no condemnation for those who belong to Christ Jesus.
And because you belong to him, the power of the life-giving
Spirit has freed you from the power of sin that leads to death.
ROMANS 8:1–2 NLT

There's a difference between same-sex attraction and committing to a homosexual or transgender lifestyle. The first is a real but misplaced desire that you can give over to God. But actively engaging in a gay or transgender relationship directly violates God's Word (1 Corinthians 6:9–10).

God's Word makes it clear that Christians should encourage anyone who struggles with sin to resist it and to follow Christ's example, rather than join in with piling on the condemnation. That is in keeping with Christ's example: "For God did not send His Son into the world to condemn the world, but that the world through Him might be saved" (John 3:17 NKJV).

God has good plans for all of us sinners (Jeremiah 29:11), which He can enact in our lives when we give ourselves completely to Him. The person struggling with homosexuality or gender identity needs love and fellowship and discipleship, just like anyone does. If this is your struggle, know that Jesus loves you. Let His goodness and mercy lead you to repentance (Romans 2:4) and realize that though your battle won't be easy, God will never give up on you or abandon you.

God, I commit myself to honoring You and to trusting You with my feelings. I pray that You will deliver me from my sinful desires. I ask this with all my heart and with expectation. I want to be included with those Paul described this way: "Some of you were once like that. But you were cleansed; you were made holy; you were made right with God by calling on the name of the Lord Jesus Christ and by the Spirit of our God" (1 Corinthians 6:11 NLT).

◇◇◇

Lord, I have prayed hard and often and asked You to take these feelings away from me. But You haven't. Remind me that You still love me, that You still have plans for me. I think of what You told Paul when he begged You to take away his physical suffering: "My grace is all you need. My power works best in weakness" (2 Corinthians 12:9 NLT). I'm grateful that You don't make mistakes, including me, and even though my body doesn't match my desires, same-sex attraction won't separate me from Your love. Strengthen me in my commitment to honoring You.

◇◇◇

Father, I can't deny my feelings, but I know that my behavior is based on a choice I make every day to follow You and flee sexual immorality (1 Corinthians 6:18). Help me resist the desires that are not Your best for me and instead embrace Your holiness, grace, and desire for purity in all my ways—the same things You want from all Your children. Give me Your abundant life (John 10:10).

Jesus, I am struggling with desires that are forbidden in Your Word, and with a culture and world that have put individual freedom as the highest possible good. I confess that sometimes I just want to do what feels right. But I give my feelings to You. You created sexuality, and You meant for it to be glorious and good, but You set it aside for marriage between a man and a woman. You alone can redeem the brokenness in me and in the world around me. Start with me, Lord. When I'm faced with temptation, let my response be like Yours—to choose the will of the Father above my own.

◇◇◇

Lord, I just found out someone I care about is struggling with his sexuality. My first impulse was to reject him, as if his struggle was somehow unpardonable. Forgive me. We all deal with our flesh and our own battles, and this struggle has got to be so hard for him. Help me to be there for him, to look past the way it makes me feel and do what You've told me to—being there for him and encouraging him to seek Your best for his life, even if it goes against his feelings.

SHAME

When pride comes, then comes dishonor, but with the humble is wisdom.
PROVERBS 11:2 NASB

Humility is hard to find in our society. In this age of selfies, we're full of ourselves. It's hard to be filled with the Holy Spirit when you're busy using a selfie stick to make sure you get the best shot. The angle has to be just right so that you look thin and attractive. Really, though, the very best angle we can hope to achieve is to see ourselves in a true light for the sinners we are. It's only by the grace of God that we are not destroyed.

God does not want us to walk around in shame. Jesus took our shame to the cross. Our sin was nailed to the cross and we bear it no more. But He does want us to walk in humility. If we are prideful, we will not gain the wisdom of our Lord. We are called to walk humbly with Him all the days of our lives.

Help me never to be ashamed of You, Jesus. I know that one day when You come again, You will be ashamed of those who are ashamed of You (Luke 9:26).

◇◇◇

I am so ashamed of my sin, Lord. It's always before me. Please remind me that when I ask You to forgive me, You are faithful to do so. I don't have to walk away hanging my head. I can stand tall. I am made righteous through my Savior's death on the cross for me. My sin is forgiven, and I can walk with confidence as a child of the living God.

◇◇◇

You are the author and perfecter of my faith. You took my shame upon Yourself and died for me. You did not stay in the grave. You sit at the right hand of God (Hebrews 12:2). You are my Savior and Redeemer. You made a way for me to be a child of God.

◇◇◇

Jesus, when You encountered disease, You saw it as simply an opportunity for Your Father to display His power through You. You knew that these physical conditions had nothing to do with sin, nor did they mean that the individual was any less worthy of respect and honor. May I have that same confidence now.

Holy Spirit, help me to let go of this sense of shame. It keeps me focused on how bad I feel about myself, and that makes me less aware of You, less sensitive to others' needs. Break down the walls of shame that enclose me, I pray. Set me free.

◇◇◇

Thank You, Christ Jesus, that there is no condemnation for those who are in You. I know that the law of the Spirit of life has set me free in You from the law of sin and death, for God has done what nothing else could do for me. By sending You to earth wearing the same sort of body that I do, God destroyed everything that separates me from Him. His righteousness is fulfilled in me, and now I can walk in the Spirit rather than in my own strength (Romans 8:1–3). I'm going to stop focusing on physical problems and set my mind on the things of Your Spirit. Help me to live by Your power.

◇◇◇

I'm ashamed to come before You. I am so sorry. I have not acted as a Christian should. I've brought disgrace to Your holy name. My iniquities have risen above my head, and my guilt has grown to the heavens (Ezra 9:6). And yet, I know that when I lay my shame before You, You reach down to me and embrace me. You're a good, good Father, and I am loved by You.

Hiding has become my norm. I avoid prayer. I fill what used to be quiet times with the noise of life. I busy myself. I don't call it hiding. I call it work and school. I call it smartphone and tablet and social media. I call it caring for children, seeing to my spouse's needs, and meeting deadlines at the office. I call it whatever I must so long as it can keep me from humbling myself before You. I'm so ashamed of who I have become.

◇◇◇

O God, in Your graciousness, peel back the layers of shame under which I have buried that part of me that walks and talks with You.

◇◇◇

Look upon me with a Jesus lens, my sin covered by His lifeblood shed for me at Calvary. It's the only way that I can show my face. He is the way, the truth, and the life. No one comes to the Father but through Him (John 14:6).

SICKNESS

The LORD sustains them on their sickbed and restores them from their bed of illness.

PSALM 41:3 NIV

No one enjoys being sick! But at one time or another, it's an experience all of us have. When sickness forces us to step back from life, to retreat to the small world of our beds, God is with us there. He will sustain us and restore us. He may even have something He wants to teach us during this time of illness!

Father, I have so much to do. How can I take time out to be sick?
I need Your healing hand, Lord. Renew my strength—
physically, emotionally, and spiritually.

◇◇◇

Jesus, in the Gospels, You healed everyone who asked for
Your help. I'm asking now: please make me better!

◇◇◇

Be with me, Lord, here in this quiet room. Let me not
feel too sick to hear what You have to say to me.

◇◇◇

Dearest Lord, heal this one I love who is sick today. You have
promised to redeem our lives from destruction, and I pray now
that You will crown this person with your loving-kindness
and tender mercies (Psalm 103:4). Thank You
that You always hear our prayers.

◇◇◇

God, I know that all circumstances can lead us to You,
even sickness. I pray that You would use this time of
pain and illness to Your greater glory.

◇◇◇

Lord, I bless You with all my soul. I will never forget all You
have done for me. You have forgiven me, You have
redeemed me, and You will heal me. (Psalm 103:2–3)

◇◇◇

Jesus, I'm sick again! I feel so frustrated with my own body.
Lord, is there something You're trying to say to me? Help me to
examine my life during this time while I'm in bed. Is my lifestyle
making me sick? Is there something You want me to change?

SINGLENESS

But each one has his own gift from God, one in this manner and another in that.
1 CORINTHIANS 7:7 NKJV

When God created the first man, He made him single. Later, He designed marriage because it was what He intended for Adam. But while Adam was in both states—married and single—God called what He made "good." So, there's nothing inherently better or worse about either state.

Some desperately want to be married and some don't. Biblically, there are reasons why a person might remain single. In Matthew 19:11–12, Jesus spoke of three types of "eunuchs"—those who stay single and celibate. Some are born "wired" to stay single, some are forced into it by external circumstances (like castration), and some choose it in order to focus wholeheartedly on kingdom work. Whatever the case, singles matter to God, and they need friends and colaborers as much as anyone else.

Not being married is not a sign of defect, nor is being single indicative of greater holiness than being married. If you're single, don't be in a hurry to get married. Seek God daily to see if He has the right person for you—or if He wants you to stay single. Also, stay connected at work and church and develop friendships. Christian fellowship should consist of singles and married couples, young and old, and men and women. If God calls you to be single, trust Him to give you the grace to live in it effectively and joyfully.

God, I admit that I often feel lonely as a single person. I try to cultivate friendships with a variety of people, but I look at married couples I know and wonder if You want me to be married. So, in a way, what I'm really feeling is frustration.

◇◇◇

Father, I am trying to be faithful in everything You've given me to do in my life—my work, ministry, and relationships.
I've had relationships with women that seem headed for marriage, but then it didn't work out. I hope it's because we both realized that it was because You didn't have a future for us and not because You really want me to be a monk or something similarly isolating. Guide me on my journey, and keep me from fear. Step-by-step, let me see You on the path ahead of me so I can know I'm headed in the right direction.

◇◇◇

Lord, as I navigate this journey of singleness, Proverbs 18:22 (NKJV) comes up a lot: "He who finds a wife finds a good thing, and obtains favor from the LORD." But then, so do Paul's words: "So I say to those who aren't married and to widows [and, I'm guessing, widowers]—it's better to stay unmarried, just as I am" (1 Corinthians 7:8 NLT). So, there are pros and cons either way. I want to focus on what You have for me now, which appears to be singleness. I'm open to Your leading, but Paul's words give me encouragement: "I want you to live as free of complications as possible. When you're unmarried, you're free to concentrate on simply pleasing the Master" (v. 32 MSG).

God, being single has its own blessings and challenges, and sex is definitely one of those challenges. Help me to resist this sex-saturated culture—it's even in the church these days!—and not be consumed with my physical urges. Sexuality is only one part of who You made me to be, but it's not the basis of the highest good I could ever experience. Guide me toward other ways I can burn off that energy and be sharpened and encouraged by other Christian single men. Above all, I want to honor You and focus on what You are doing now and not on what I am not experiencing. What looks like "lack" in the world's eyes is an opening to a fruitful life, a life fully committed to You.

◇◇◇

Jesus, I commit to truly loving others the way You did. I want to seek the highest good of those You bring into my life, focusing not on the "don'ts" of singleness but the "dos" of following Christ. Help me to maintain appropriate and respectful boundaries in my relationships, especially with the opposite sex—particularly with emotional intimacy, which, along with physical intimacy, You've reserved for marriage. Let Your Word guide me: "Everyone who believes that Jesus is the Christ has become a child of God. And everyone who loves the Father loves his children, too. We know we love God's children if we love God and obey his commandments" (1 John 5:1–2 NLT).

SURGERY

*Don't panic. I'm with you. There's no need to fear for I'm your God. . . .
I'll hold you steady, keep a firm grip on you.*
ISAIAH 41:10 MSG

As we face a surgery, our hearts are often filled with fear. This procedure forces us to acknowledge we cannot control our lives. We must surrender to our doctors, trusting the outcome to them. . . and to God. We go under anesthesia, uncertain what we will find when we wake up. It seems a little like death, a venture into a dark and unknown place!

But God's hands are sure. He holds us safe. He will never let us drop, neither in this life nor in the one to come.

Strengthen me in mind, body, and soul to face this surgery. Give my doctors sharp minds and steady hands, and guide them if they come up short. I want to be at my best as soon as possible so I can go on with the work You have for me. You have given me new life in Christ, and You are the healer and sustainer of my soul. Heal my body as well, Father, and glorify Your name in the process.

◇◇◇

Lord, I place my body in Your hands today. Guide the medical professionals who will work on my body. Give them skill and wisdom, sure hands and alert minds. Use them to restore me to health, that You may be glorified.

◇◇◇

Give me the courage, Jesus, to say the words You spoke on the cross: "Into Your hands I commit my spirit" (Luke 23:46 NIV).

◇◇◇

As I go into the operating room, I will rest in Your promises, loving Lord. I will lean back into Your love for me, sinking into Your peace as the surgeons work. Remind me that You are there with them, in them. I know that when I am most vulnerable, You will be with me, that Your love will hold me safe.

◇◇◇

Jesus, my best friend, You know how scared I am as I face this surgery. What if something goes wrong? What if there are complications? Will I ever feel like myself again? How much pain will I have to face during the recovery process? In the midst of all these fears, Lord, I cling to You. Yes, I'm terrified—but I nevertheless trust You.

Please be with me during this surgery. Breathe Your peace
into my heart. Be with my family as they wait.
Assure them that You are in control.

◇◇◇

Jesus, may the doctors and nurses who care for me today,
before and after the surgery, sense Your presence
in me. Bless them through me, I pray.

◇◇◇

God of power and might, guide the surgeon's hands, I pray.
May our loved one's body respond quickly to this treatment.
May this person we love be healed to serve You anew.

◇◇◇

Lord, I place my loved one in Your hands today. Guide the
medical professionals who will do the surgery. Give them skill
and wisdom, sure hands and alert minds. Use them to
restore health so that You may be glorified.

◇◇◇

Lord, You told us not to worry about tomorrow. Thank You
that You pour out Your Spirit upon us anew each day, even on
days like this one. Thank You that Your grace is sufficient
for us in each moment that we live, even this moment
as we face surgery (2 Corinthians 12:9).

◇◇◇

As I lie on the operating table, may I know Your peace in my
heart, Jesus, a peace that surpasses all understanding,
that will guard my heart and mind (Philippians 4:7).

Holy Spirit, as I undergo this surgery, come and be present with
me, watching and waiting, ready to help and guard me every
moment during this procedure. Hold me in Your love,
and protect me from all harm.

◇◇◇

Lord, my loved one is facing surgery. Be his peace right now as
You strengthen his body and prepare his mind and spirit.
Give his doctors the greatest skill possible and guide the
outcome toward the highest possible good. Would You help
him to recover quickly and be better off because of this
operation? Thank You, Lord, for my dear one.
I lift him up to You in Jesus' name.

◇◇◇

God, I am leaning into Your arms as I face this operation.
Protect me and help this surgery to go well. The thought of You
being with me when I am at my weakest gives me comfort.

◇◇◇

Lord, You are the Author of Life, the Great Healer. You know
all that is wrong inside my body. Please be with me during this
surgery. Breathe Your peace into my heart. Be with my family
as they wait. Assure them that You are in control.

◇◇◇

Lord, I face this surgery with expectation, hope, and faith.
I'm focused on these words You've given me: "And the prayer
offered in faith will make the sick person well; the Lord will
raise them up. If they have sinned, they will be forgiven" (James
5:15 NIV). Bring to my mind anything I need to confess and any
person with whom I need to make things right, bringing Your
healing on a spiritual level in advance of bringing
it on a physical one. I put my trust in You.

TERROR

*I am so bewildered I cannot hear, so terrified I cannot see.
My mind reels, horror overwhelms me.*

Isaiah 21:3–4 NASB

Fear is a normal and healthy biological reaction that alerts us to danger. By flooding our bodies with adrenaline, making our heartbeat increase and our breath come faster, fear was designed to prepare our bodies either to run away or take action. But when facing the reality of an impossible situation, we can do neither of those things. We can't run away; we don't know how to take action. We feel helpless. We find ourselves frozen with terror—unable to hear, see, speak, or think.

That reaction is normal. As we move forward on this new path, the terror will retreat. But for now, simply know that God is still present. He is still our refuge. He is big enough to hold our fear, and He will never leave us.

You are my light and salvation, Lord. You are my stronghold, so I will not fear anything! (Psalm 27:1).

◇◇◇

You are with me, Lord, so I won't be afraid. What can anything on earth do to me when I have You? (Psalm 118:6).

◇◇◇

You didn't give me a terrified spirit, God, but a spirit of power, of love, and of self-discipline (2 Timothy 1:7).

◇◇◇

Send Your angel to encamp around me, loving Lord. Deliver me (Psalm 34:7).

◇◇◇

Heavenly Father, I know You don't want me to be in bondage to fear. And because Your Spirit has adopted me, I can cry, "Daddy! Father!"—and I know You'll hear me! (Romans 8:15).

◇◇◇

Help me to hear Your voice saying to me, "Fear not, for I have redeemed you; I have called you by name, you are mine" (Isaiah 43:1 ESV).

Lord, You are my light and my salvation. Whom shall I fear? You are the strength of my life. Of whom shall I be afraid? When my enemies attack me, they'll stumble and fall. Though an entire army of fears comes against me, my heart will be strong. Even facing the reality of my situation, I can be confident in You, because I ask You for only one thing: that I may dwell in Your house all the days of my life, seeing Your beauty. For I know that now, in this time of trouble, You will hide me in Your pavilion. You'll tuck me away in a secret nook inside Your tabernacle; You'll set me on a rock where I'll be safe, where I can lift up my head and see beyond this terror. And that's why, Lord, I sing to You with joy—even now! (Psalm 27:1–6).

◇◇◇

When we heard the diagnosis, our hearts melted in fear and everyone's courage failed. But we know that the Lord our God is God in heaven above and on the earth below. So I pray, dear Lord, that You will show kindness to my family. Give me confidence that You will be with us all—parents, grandparents, children, brothers, and sisters—and all who care about us—and that You will save us from death (Joshua 2:11–12).

◇◇◇

Jesus, I hear Your voice telling me not to be afraid. *"Look!"* You say. *"I'll care for everyone who travels with you on this journey. So take courage."* I believe You, Jesus. I trust that it will happen just as You say (Acts 27:24–25).

TOXIC FRIENDSHIPS

*Then Jonathan and David made a covenant,
because he loved him as his own soul.*

1 Samuel 18:3 ASV

The friendship between Jonathan and David was a healthy one. It fulfilled the Golden Rule, for each treated the other as he would choose to be treated himself. David loved Jonathan as much as he loved himself.

Friendships become toxic, however, when they no longer have this quality of healthy love. Instead, the relationship becomes destructive. One side uses and manipulates the other.

Often this situation can creep up on us. We may not realize how unhealthy and poisonous a relationship has become until the problem is bigger than we know how to handle. Even once we recognize the problem, we may not know what to do. As Christians, we may feel guilty setting boundaries. We may think that God would want us to sacrifice ourselves to this damaging situation.

God never wants us to be involved in something that isn't healthy for us, though. When we find ourselves involved in a toxic friendship, we need to ask Him to show us the way to freedom—for our sake, for the sake of our friend, and for His sake as well. He is not glorified by a relationship that damages and destroys!

Lord, give me wisdom to recognize when a friendship is no longer healthy. I know that true friends support one another. They help each other overcome adversity. They help each other feel good about themselves. They accept one another unconditionally. They reflect Your love to each other. When I find myself involved with a relationship that doesn't have these qualities, give me the courage to make a change.

◇◇◇

Jesus, I realize that after I've been with this friend, I often feel less sure of myself. I feel ashamed, embarrassed, less confident. That can't be what You want! Remind me to rely on Your love for my self-worth. Don't let me hand my identity over to this toxic relationship.

◇◇◇

Heavenly Father, sometimes I feel like You want me to sacrifice myself to this friend. I feel like I should be a "good Christian" and just take the abuse. I know that's not a thought that comes from You. Help me to stand against Satan's schemes. You do not want your child to be treated poorly time and time again. Help me to know how to find freedom from this friendship that is so disheartening.

◇◇◇

Jesus, this friend brings me down. After we spend time together, I don't feel good about myself. This friend has a way of subtly knocking me down in order to build up self. Give me words to speak so that I can convey my feelings to this person. If I am met with refusal to be heard, give me wisdom, Father, on whether to walk away from this friendship or attempt to continue it.

Lord, thank You that You always listen to me. Lead me to a friendship that will provide an equal give-and-take.

◇◇◇

God, she's jealous. I see it in her eyes. I hear it in her snide comments. I don't know why she's so envious of my life. It's not like I have a perfect existence. I think she just sees certain ways You've blessed me and she wants these things for herself. She doesn't seem like a friend, Father. This seems more like an enemy. Help me to know how to handle this situation. How did I get so entrenched with someone who is not good for me?

◇◇◇

God, You tell me in Your Word to guard my heart, for it is the wellspring of life. I didn't do that. I opened up to someone who wasn't safe. I wasn't sure at the time, but now I see that it was a big mistake. This person has not been a faithful friend and has repeated things I shared in confidence and gossiped about me. It's so hard to know what to do. Show me whether to confront my friend, I pray. Give me a forgiving spirit toward this person, but give me wisdom so that I will not place trust in unsafe people again.

◇◇◇

I found out that my friend has been gossiping about me, God. Talking about me behind my back. Sharing my confidences with people without my permission. How could someone betray my trust like that? Lord Jesus, I know I've let You down in so many ways. Help me not to be self-righteous. Help me to forgive— but at the same time, help me to learn not to share my heart so openly with someone who has proven untrustworthy.

Lord, will You provide a new friendship for me? Will You place on my path a friend who will not do all the taking and all the talking? I need someone to listen to me sometimes, to care about my problems, to help me. I am tired of being the giver 100 percent of the time.

◇◇◇

Lord, he did it again. He broke his promises to me. He let me down. I feel like such an idiot. Show me what to do now. Should I confront him? Should I let him know I can't trust him again? What would You do in my place? Please give me Your wisdom.

◇◇◇

Thank You, Lord, for Your faithful friendship. You never leave me. You are always there. Even when I have strayed, You are still there waiting when I come to my senses. I love You, Lord.

◇◇◇

God, it seems like this friendship started out okay, but things have changed. Help me to accept that not all friendships last a lifetime. It may be time to walk away from this one.

◇◇◇

God, I feel so lonely. I've spent an entire day with my friend, but all I've done is listen to her talk about her life. I don't want to be selfish, Lord—but I had a problem I wanted to share with someone, and she refused to listen. I felt like all she wanted from me was to be a sounding board for her voice, chattering on and on about trivial things. I feel angry—and I feel guilty for resenting her.

UNFORGIVENESS

And Jesus said, Father, forgive them; for they know not what they do.
LUKE 23:34 ASV

◆

It's not always easy to forgive. If we are Christ's followers, however, we must follow His example. If He could forgive the people who were killing Him, we can certainly find a way to forgive those who hurt us!

Ultimately, when we can't forgive, we hurt ourselves more than anyone. Nursing a grudge damages our own hearts. It can even make us physically ill.

God wants to set us free from old grievances and harbored resentments. He will heal our wounded hearts and give us the strength to forgive. After all, He forgave us, didn't He?

Lord, I have spent too much time keeping accounts of wrong done against me. I felt justified in doing so, but I now understand that I've only been adding to an oppressive weight on my soul. The Bible says vengeance is Yours, and You will pay people back for their wrongdoing—me included (Hebrews 10:30). You have better things for me to focus on than paying people back. Forgive me for the energy I've put into my anger and hardheartedness. I will forgive those who have wronged me because You forgave me.

◇◇◇

Lord Jesus, if You could forgive the people who stripped You and drove nails through Your hands and feet, who hung You upon the cross to die, then I know You can help me to forgive those who have offended or wronged me.

◇◇◇

God, free me of resentment and self-righteousness. Take the two-by-four out my own eye before I worry too much about the speck in someone else's! Make me humble enough to forgive.

◇◇◇

Jesus, in the Gospels, You always showed mercy to the sinners. But You had no patience for the proud and unforgiving Pharisees.

◇◇◇

God, I know You want me to live at peace with others—but I won't be able to do that until I can forgive. Help me forgive that which seems unforgiveable. Free my heart so that I can be at peace with everyone.

Lord, may I carry Your forgiveness to all who have hurt me.
May they see You in me. Work Your reconciliation through me.

◇◇◇

God, I've struggled to forgive certain people. I've made all sorts of justifications for not doing so, but in the end, I'm just angry and hurt. I can feel my pain growing in me like a weed, and I need Your help to root it out. I know that starts with me forgiving those who have hurt me. I'm sorry for forgetting all You have forgiven me for. Forgiveness is based on Your character and the redeeming work of Christ at the cross. I leave my anger and pain there.
Fill the void with Your grace, mercy, and forgiveness,
so I can extend to others what You first gave me.

◇◇◇

Father, I've been like the Pharisee who criticized Jesus for letting the woman wash His feet with perfume and her hair. He called her a sinner, and Jesus didn't disagree but said, "Her many sins have been forgiven—as her great love has shown. But whoever has been forgiven little loves little" (Luke 7:47 NIV). By Your grace, help me to love my enemies, and so release myself
from the bitterness of unforgiveness.

◇◇◇

Jesus, in failing to forgive, I've cut myself off from forgiveness. Your Word says, "Forgive others, and you will be forgiven" (Luke 6:37 NLT). I've been seeing myself as a victim, but that only hurts me and others who have done me no wrong. I'm trusting You that when I do forgive, You'll guide me to the core cause of my stubbornness—self-defense, fear, mistrust, unreasonable expectations, whatever it may be. Bring about fresh starts in these relationships—renewal of trust
and reconciliation—and let that start with me.

VIOLENCE

*Jesus said, "Put your sword back where it belongs.
All who use swords are destroyed by swords."*
MATTHEW 26:52 MSG

By our own standards, Peter would have been perfectly justified in using his sword to defend Jesus. But Christ calls us to a different standard. One of our greatest challenges as His followers is to walk His path of peace in the midst of a violent world.

Violence bombards us from all directions. It comes at us on the news, in movies, and on television. Violence touches our schools and our workplaces. We see it on our highways, we run into it in stores. It's evident at the national and global level—and it even comes into our homes.

We may think we have no part in this violence, but Jesus calls us to examine our hearts. He reminds us that if our thoughts are full of rage and hatred, then we too nurse the roots of violence inside our very beings. He asks us instead to become His hands and feet on this earth, spreading His peace.

Lord, I believe that if I'm in Christ, I'm a new creation. The old things have passed away and all things have become new (2 Corinthians 5:17). Take all violent thoughts away from me. Make me a new creature.

◇◇◇

"Lord make me an instrument of Your peace. Where there is hatred, let me sow love. Where there is injury, pardon. Where there is doubt, faith. Where there is despair, hope. Where there is darkness, light. Where there is sadness, joy. O Divine Master, grant that I may not so much seek to be consoled, as to console. To be understood, as to understand, to be loved, as to love. For it is in giving that we receive, it is in pardoning that we are pardoned, and it is in dying that we are born to eternal life" (Prayer of Francis of Assisi).

◇◇◇

Lord, the time is coming when I will suffer for following You (John 15:18–21), perhaps even violently. If it doesn't happen on a societal or global scale, it will happen on a personal level. Help me to face it the way Jesus did, looking to accomplish Your will before His own desire to avoid pain and suffering. He is my example: "For God called you to do good, even if it means suffering, just as Christ suffered for you" (1 Peter 2:21 NLT).

Jesus, violence is part of this broken world. Because of that, I should never embrace it as something You support or justify—even if it is a necessity in certain situations. Let me not misapply Your Word and will to justify my behavior, but let me be guided by You in all I do. You died for all of us, and You don't want anyone to live apart from You. But You always give us the choice. And for me, even though I'm redeemed, You allow me to choose to seek You above all else. Let Your motives for interacting with people, for defending the weak and poor and helpless, be my motives.

◇◇◇

Jesus, You left Your peace with us. The peace You give is not like the world's. We don't need to be worried or afraid (John 14:27). We need never resort to violence.

◇◇◇

If I have bitter envy and self-seeking in my heart, Lord, You tell me that I am lying against Your truth. This is not Your way of doing things, but the world's. For when envy and self-seeking fill my heart, I have opened the door to confusion and violence. Your way of doing things is far different! It's based on peace and gentleness. When I do things Your way, I'm willing to yield my way to another's; I'm full of mercy for everyone; I don't show favoritism; and I'm free of hypocrisy. The fruit of Your righteousness is sown in peace when I become Your peacemaker. (James 3:14–18)

God, I acknowledge my own natural (that is, broken and sinful) tendencies toward violence. My heart has held onto bitterness, lust, anger, and greed, and harsh words have flowed from my mouth because of those things. These are all forms of violence. You warned Cain that if he didn't master his sinful desires, they would master him (Genesis 4:6–7). He didn't, and they did, to his great shame and His brother's death. Cleanse my heart of all iniquity.

◇◇◇

Lord, when the blood of innocents cries out to me, it's hard not to at least think about a violent response. But You have said that vengeance is Yours, that You will repay wrongdoing (Hebrews 10:30). I want to obey You in serving the poor and oppressed, but I want to do it out of love, not out of anger and fear. If I must use violence to defend my family or to protect innocents in dangerous and unstable parts of the world, let me not justify it as Your perfect will but as a necessity in a broken world.

◇◇◇

Father, when I realize that violence and violation have the same roots, I understand better how careful I need to be to walk Your path of peace. Any time I violate another's trust, whenever I trespass on another rights, I am committing a form of violence. Make me careful to always treat others with Your respect.

Jesus, when I look at the world, I feel helpless to counteract the violence I see everywhere. But let me take the first step: I give You my own heart to change. Take out the greed and bitterness and unforgiveness I hold inside. Fill me instead with peace, goodwill, and kindness for everyone. May I, like Your cousin John, prepare the way of the Lord.

◇◇◇

Father, You have called me to peace. Because You are my peace, and because You desire reconciliation with anyone who would come to You, I turn from pursuing even the thought of violence as a way to achieve justice. That's Your job. Violence is part of this fallen world, but it should never be anything but the last resort. I pray for those whose job it is to be peacemakers, that You would give them wisdom and help them to build a greater sense of unity in our communities and world. Help me to be aware of anyone around me who might be hurting and looking to hurt others, and give me the courage and the words to reach out before they make a terrible decision.

WEAKNESS

But those who trust in the Lord will find new strength. They will soar high on wings like eagles. They will run and not grow weary. They will walk and not faint.
Isaiah 40:31 NLT

There are so many demands on our strength. So many crises to confront, so many problems to solve, so many people who need our help. We feel exhausted. We're not sure we can go on. Some days, we'd like to just give up. We've reached the end of our strength.

But when we acknowledge our own weakness, that's the moment when the Holy Spirit can begin to work in our lives in new ways. When we throw up our own hands, God's hands have room to work.

God, I am worn out. So many things have been happening that require my care and attention, but somehow I let my busyness push my need for You out of the picture. It's no wonder I'm so frustrated and weak. But here I am, snapping out of it. I need You, Lord. Your grace is enough for me. I know You will give me what I need—the rest, the wisdom, the will— to keep seeking You as life rolls on.

◇◇◇

Heavenly Father, make me strong in You. May my strength come from Your might (Ephesians 6:10).

◇◇◇

I want to soar as the eagles. I watch them, God. They take flight and so gracefully soar above the earth. I want my spirit to be light and free again. I feel so powerless in this situation. I am weak, but You are strong. Be my strength today. I ask this in the strong name of Your Son, Jesus.

◇◇◇

Today I pray that You will go before me. In every moment of weakness, I pray You will show up to provide supernatural strength. Where I am failing, bring success. Where I am losing my grip, take hold. Where I am discouraged, lift me up. I will trust in You.

Some trust in chariots or horses. I trust in the name of the
Lord my God (Psalm 20:7). I choose to walk in the strength
of my Savior. I choose to rest in my Redeemer. I choose
to endure because of Emmanuel—God with us.
God before me. God with me. God beside me.

◇◇◇

"Lord Jesus Christ, King of kings, You have power over life and
death. You know even things that are uncertain and obscure,
and our very thoughts and feelings are not hidden from You.
Cleanse me from my secret faults. . . . You know how weak
I am, both in soul and in body. Give me strength, O Lord, in
my frailty and sustain me in my sufferings. Grant me a
prudent judgment, dear Lord, and let me always be
mindful of Your blessings" (Ephrem of Syria).

◇◇◇

Father, I spend so much time trying to decide which is the good,
which is the better, and which is the best. I'm juggling too many
things. I need Your discernment, Your wisdom, and Your
perspective to determine what is best—that is, whatever You want
me to do next. Teach me how to say no. Help me figure out
what to let go of and what to hold on to. You know
what's best for me and the people in my life.

Lord, You see my weaknesses. You know the areas where
I struggle. But I can do all things through You
who gives me strength (Philippians 4:13).

◇◇◇

Lord, when David wrote Psalm 102, he subtitled it: "A Prayer
of one afflicted, when he is faint and pours out his complaint
before the LORD" (ESV). As I read it aloud, please accept it as my
prayer too. I need You, and I know You won't let me down.

◇◇◇

Jesus, I need Your help. It's hard to even describe everything
I'm feeling. I'm overwhelmed, disappointed, exhausted,
and anxious, but I give it all to You. Thank You that You are
at God's right hand right now, interceding for me in prayer
(Hebrews 7:25). Give me Your grace, and help me to
extend it to others, especially to those who
are part of the issues I'm facing.

WORRY

*Don't worry about anything; instead, pray about everything.
Tell God what you need, and thank him for all he has done.*

PHILIPPIANS 4:6 NLT

◆

All of us worry. We worry about the future. We worry about our weight. We worry about our family. We worry about money. We worry about work responsibilities. Worry, worry, worry! The list of worries is endless.

Guess what the Old German root word of *worry* is? It's "to strangle"! Worries strangle us. They make it so we can't breathe in the Spirit of God. They twist our minds out of the healthy shape God wants them to have. Worries interfere with the flow of God's life into ours.

But our worries can be turned into prayers. Each time a worry occurs to us, we need to form the habit of lifting it up to God. As we offer our worries to Him, they will lose their stranglehold on our lives. And then we will find ourselves instead thanking God for all He has done.

God, my thoughts are a train wreck—car after car full of care after care, all banging into each other. I know a lot of it is relatively trivial, but the little things I worry about become bigger issues surrounding the decisions I've made or the people those decisions have affected. I'm calling time out and coming to You with all of it. You care about all the details of my life, and I'm counting on Your peace—which is far beyond my understanding—to keep my mind and thoughts on You and not on my worries (Philippians 4:6–7).

◇◇◇

Jesus, remind me that You are not only with me but in me: "It is no longer I who live, but Christ lives in me. So I live in this earthly body by trusting in the Son of God, who loved me and gave himself for me" (Galatians 2:20 NLT). You didn't save me from the worst possible fate—eternal separation from God—just to leave me hanging on all these comparatively smaller details. You are my peace.

◇◇◇

God, I give You my present and my future because I know You can handle them better than I ever could. You have shown up in my past and provided for my every need. You have filled my life with blessings. Help me to trust You with the unknown by banking on what I do know—You are a faithful God.

Because I dwell in the secret place of the Most High, Lord, I shall abide under the shadow of the Almighty. I do not need to worry in the night, nor do I need to fret about dangers during the day. Neither sickness nor destruction are my concern. Even though people all around me are in trouble, I still don't need to worry, because You are my refuge. You—the Most High—are my dwelling place. You have given Your angels the job of looking after me. No matter what dangers I face, I am safe. Because of Your love, You will deliver me. You will set me in a high place. When I call on You, You answer me. If trouble comes, You will still be with me. You will deliver me and honor me. You will show me Your salvation all through my life. So why should I worry? (Psalm 91)

◇◇◇

Lord, thank You for all You've done for me. You've blessed me with all I need, especially in my relationship with You in Christ. There's so much I can't control, but this is something I can do: seek You, thank You, praise You, and ask for Your help. Comfort me, Holy Spirit, and bring to mind all the things I need to recall right now about Your goodness and provision (John 14:26–27).

◇◇◇

Lord, You are in complete control—and You are greater than any of my worries. I cannot change the future, I cannot change human hearts, I may not be able to change the circumstances of my life—so worrying is simply a waste of time and energy! Teach me that my energy could be better spent in prayer.

You are a big God. You are bigger than all the little things I worry about. You are bigger than Satan who tries to drag me down with anxiety and fear. I claim the name of Jesus, and I pray for power to fight against the spiritual forces that battle daily against Christians.

◇◇◇

Lord, You are Jehovah-Jireh (the Lord will provide). You provided a ram for Abraham to sacrifice in place of his beloved son Isaac. You provided right at the moment that a sacrifice was needed. Thank You for the assurance that You will provide for my needs as well. I can trust You all of my life—in every stage, at every crossroads. I will trust in my Provider.

◇◇◇

You are with me and You are for me. If God is for me, who can be against me? What will it matter if they are? No one is stronger than my God.

◇◇◇

Lord, like a mother hen protecting her chicks, You protect Your children (Psalm 91:4). I have no reason to worry or fear. You are always with me, watching over me, and laying out the path before me one step at a time. You don't give me more than I can handle. You created me and You know me better than I even know myself. I trust You, God.

God, You showed up for Daniel in the lions' den. You have proven time and time again in my own life that You always come through for Your children. You know what we need and when we need it. This life is a journey, and it's a lesson in trust. Help me to be a scholar who learns the lessons early so that I am not worrying my years away.

◇◇◇

I'm struggling under the weight of a burden You could carry with ease. The problem is You won't fight me for it. You tell me to cast my cares upon You. You ask me to trust You and to lean not on my own understanding (Proverbs 3:5). You tell me that Your ways are higher than my ways (Isaiah 55:8–9) and that You know the plans You have for me (Jeremiah 29:11). And yet, I struggle under the weight of worry. Help me, Father, not to just pay lip service to surrender but to truly surrender. I keep picking the worries back up. Help me to deposit them fully and forever at the foot of Your throne. You are strong enough and wise enough to handle all of my concerns.

◇◇◇

Thank You, Father, for giving me the confidence that You are for me and with me. I know that life holds nothing that You can't overcome. No power is greater than You. I can rest in Your arms today, knowing that You have everything under control.

Father, You have not given me a spirit of fear, "but of power and of love and of a sound mind" (2 Timothy 1:7 NKJV). Worry is not from You, God, but from my fear and lack of faith. I will trust You because You are my God, and I know You love me. I humble myself under Your hand, knowing that You will lift me up in Your good timing. I trust Your Word: "Live carefree before God; he is most careful with you" (1 Peter 5:7 MSG).

◇◇◇

Lord, I'm imagining that You are a mother hen, and I'm a chick (Psalm 91:4). I've crawled under Your wing. Your feathers are all around me. I have nothing to worry about.

◇◇◇

Loving Jesus, You know all the worries that flood my thoughts. I feel helpless to stem their tide. All I can do is ask You for help. I realize, Lord, that when I worry, I'm trying to hold on to my own control over my life. I don't want to let go and accept that You may have other ideas. I want to make things happen the way I want them to happen. I don't trust You to be able to handle things on my own. It's as though You were carrying a suitcase that hardly weighed anything from Your perspective—and I was a little ant running alongside You, saying, "Let me carry it! I can carry it better! Let me! Let me!" Lord, forgive me. I ask for Your will to be done in Your way in Your time. I trust You. I give You all my worries.

More Devotionals for Difficult Times...

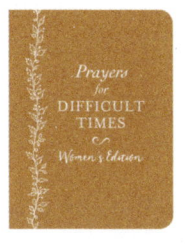

Prayers for Difficult Times Women's Edition
Here's a practical guide of short prayer starters that will help women pray confidently during difficult times. From illness and relationship issues to struggles with self-esteem and daily life stresses, dozens of topics are covered. Each section opens with a short devotional thought and applicable scripture.

DiCarta / 978-1-68322-210-1 / $12.99

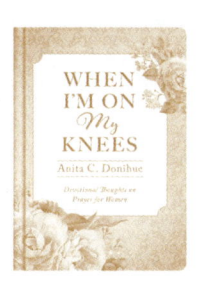

When I'm On My Knees
When I'm on My Knees has blessed more than a million readers since its 1997 release, and now it's available in a beautiful 20th anniversary edition! With themes like praise, forgiveness, healing, trials, love, God's faithfulness, and worship, Anita Corrine Donihue's encouraging devotional thoughts will touch all aspects of your life.

Hardback / 978-1-68322-484-6 / $12.99

Find These and More from Barbour Publishing
at Your Favorite Bookstore or at
www.barbourbooks.com

BARBOUR PUBLISHING